TIPS FOR IMPROVING TESTING AND GRADING

SURVIVAL SKILLS FOR SCHOLARS

Managing Editor: Peter Labella

Survival Skills for Scholars provides you, the professor or advanced graduate student working in a college or university setting, with practical suggestions for making the most of your academic career. These brief, readable guides will help you with skills that you are required to master as a college professor but may have never been taught in graduate school. Using hands-on, jargon-free advice and examples, forms, lists, and suggestions for additional resources, experts on different aspects of academic life give invaluable tips on managing the day-to-day tasks of academia—effectively and efficiently.

Volumes in This Series

SURVIVAL SKILLS FOR SCHOLARS

TIPS FOR IMPROVING TESTING AND GRADING

JOHN C. ORY

KATHERINE E. RYAN

SAGE Publications

International Educational and Professional Publisher

Newbury Park London New Delhi

For information address:

SAGE Publications, Inc.
2455 Teller Road
Newbury Park, California 91320
E-mail: order@sagepub.com

SAGE Publications Ltd.
6 Bonhill Street
London EC2A 4PU
United Kingdom

SAGE Publications India Pvt. Ltd.
M-32 Market
Greater Kailash I
New Delhi 110 048 India

Printed in the United States of America

Library of Congress Cataloging-in-Publication Data

Ory, John C.
   Tips for improving testing and grading / John C. Ory, Katherine E. Ryan.
       p.   cm.   — (Survival skills for scholars ; vol. 4)
   Includes bibliographical references.
   ISBN 0-8039-4973-1. — ISBN 0-8039-4974-X (pbk.)
   1. Examinations—United States—Design and construction.
2. Educational tests and measurements—United States.   Grading
and marking (Students)—United States.   I. Ryan, Katherine E.
II. Title. III. Series.
LB3060.65.O75   1993
371.2'61—dc20   93-24838
                                                                  CIP
97 98 99 00 01 02 03 9 8 7 6 5 4 3

Sage Production Editor: Yvonne Könneker

Contents

Introduction

D_{o you . . .}

- Test your students with the same tests that you took as a student?
- Gloss over student complaints about your tests on the basis that all students complain about testing?
- Use the same tests and test items each semester without evaluating their quality?
- List student scores from the lowest to the highest and assign grades based on "natural" gaps?

Although these approaches may get the job done, there are other more effective ways to assess student learning. For 30 years our university testing office has presented practical suggestions for effective classroom assessment by conducting hundreds of faculty workshops. In this book we combine our training materials with our experience working with faculty to provide a resource for developing, using, and grading classroom exams. If you are a new instructor, we want to help you develop effective assessment strategies. We also want to encourage those of you with classroom experience to reevaluate your testing and grading procedures.

Through the years many instructors have told us that teaching is more fun than testing and that anything is more fun

1

than grading. We realize it takes a significant amount of time and effort to develop fair and accurate assessment procedures. Yet, we encourage you to spend as much time developing exams and grading papers as you do preparing classroom presentations, because there are multiple benefits to be gained by your efforts.

First, you can be assured that you worked as hard assigning fair and accurate grades as most of your students worked earning them. Second, well-written exams can be used by students to determine what content they have mastered and what knowledge they have failed to understand. They can use their exam performance to determine what content they need to review before moving on to more difficult material. Third, you can assess the quality of your teaching by analyzing the mistakes of your students. Do their weaknesses represent yours? Are there content areas that could be better presented or more clearly explained?

We hope that you can use our suggestions for developing exams and assigning grades to get more out of each activity. Testing and grading may not be fun things to do, but they are important teaching activities that deserve your attention and best efforts.

Chapters 1 through 4 cover the development of a classroom exam, from content selection to item writing. Chapter 1 addresses ways for you to determine what content should be included on an exam and at what level of understanding. Chapter 2 identifies testing considerations—such as number of exams, difficulty level of items, and test length—that you should address before writing test items. Chapters 3 and 4 provide guidelines for writing different types of test questions, including multiple choice, true-false, matching, essays, short answer, and problem sets. A well-written test item should be answered correctly by students who have acquired the targeted content rather than by students without content knowledge but who have mastered test-taking skills or have particular abilities or traits that are beneficial in some test-taking situations, for example, risk taking and writing ability. Examples of "good" and "bad" items are provided for each item type.

Chapter 5 covers how to assemble a test with a special emphasis on preparing a professional-looking exam. Suggestions about test directions, test administration, and dealing with cheating are also offered. Several issues related to scoring objective and constructed response items are discussed. Chapter 6 presents information on how to evaluate the quality of individual test items and the test as a whole. Suggestions on how to deal with common test problems are presented. Also discussed are ways that you can determine if there are content areas that were not adequately taught or assessed. Recommendations about handling student questions about the exam and how to review the exam with the class are presented.

Chapter 7 takes up grading issues for you to consider when developing your grading strategy. A set of guidelines developed for the college or university setting is presented along with a discussion of the strengths and weaknesses of common grading methods are presented. Finally, in Chapter 8 we review all of the testing and grading activities presented in the book and describe them in terms of a developmental process.

1 | Testing What You Want to Be Testing

Developing and Using Course Objectives

How do you decide what to include on a classroom test? Many instructors scan their class notes and reading materials and look at major topics covered. You take out old exams and search for good items. You may even examine the item bank or instructor's manual provided with the text. Whatever strategy is used, you are consistently asking yourself one question, "Is this something the student should know at this point in the course?" Although you may not realize it, you are formulating course objectives as you answer this single question time and time again.

Are you reluctant to specify course objectives because you see it as a difficult and time-consuming task? It doesn't have to be either. We are speaking of course objectives that are simple statements of desired student change. For example, the student should be able to . . .

- Name three carbohydrates
- Compute a standard deviation
- Balance chemical equations
- Give an example of an oxymoron
- Explain the role of positive reinforcement in operant conditioning
- Compare single- and double-blind research designs

Objectives indicate behaviors and skills that students should be able to do after preparing for class, listening to the lecture, and completing the homework. They are easy to write and take a minimum amount of time to create, especially if you take a few minutes to do so after developing and delivering each lecture presentation. Objectives written for each lecture can be combined to guide the development of classroom exams. Test items can be written, taken from old exams, or selected from available item banks to cover each of the desired outcomes. You can make additional use of course objectives by distributing them to your classes to guide the study preparation of your students.

Activity: Try writing objectives by taking one of your recent lectures and developing three or four objectives that identify your expectations of your students.

Assessing Different Levels of Learning

Some instructors complain about writing objectives because they believe simple statements indicate simple behaviors. This obviously is not the case as can be seen by the list of sample objectives given above. Abilities to compare, to compute, and to balance equations are not acts done by the mere recall of facts. Instructional objectives can be written at different levels of learning. Several taxonomies or hierarchies of learning have been developed in response to the critics of instructional objectives. One of the best known and most used was developed by Bloom and a committee of colleagues. The Taxonomy of Educational Objectives is a classification scheme for writing objectives that measure all possible learning outcomes that might be expected of students.

What has become known as Bloom's Taxonomy views the learning process as climbing a ladder of learning outcome rungs. A student can only get to the top level of learning by successfully completing the lower levels. The taxonomy can be used to categorize instructional objectives into a hierarchy of six learning levels, starting with simple knowledge outcomes and proceeding through the increasingly complex levels of comprehension, application, analysis, synthesis, and evaluation. The hierarchy is progressive in that achievement of comprehension objectives relies on the successful completion of knowledge-level objectives; achievement at the application level is possible only after successful completion of knowledge and comprehension objectives, and so on. The following is a brief description of the expected cognitive behavior at the six levels of the taxonomy.

Knowledge. The ability to know specific facts, common terms, basic concepts, and principles.

Comprehension. The ability to understand, to interpret, to compare and contrast, to translate, to estimate, and to explain.

Application. The ability to apply previously learned facts and concepts to new situations, to solve problems, and to construct charts and figures.

Analysis. The ability to distinguish between facts and inferences, to recognize faulty assumptions in an argument, and to identify the organizational structure of something (art, music, and writing).

Synthesis. The ability to create something like a well-written essay or a beautiful piece of art, to propose an action plan, to formulate a new scheme for classifying objects, and to integrate many ideas into one solution.

Evaluation. The ability to judge the quality of something based on its adequacy, value, logic, or use.

When we work with instructors on issues of test construction we always begin with a discussion of Bloom's Taxonomy. We encourage instructors to write course objectives at different learning levels and to use the taxonomy to analyze their teaching process, their desired student outcomes, and their test items (Figure 1.1). There is cause for concern if all three components are not in agreement. If you expect students to

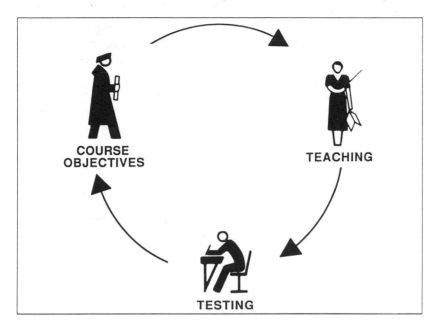

Figure 1.1. Cycle of Agreement Among Course Objectives, Teaching, and Testing

perform at a particular taxonomic level you need to aim your teaching to that level. You cannot expect your students to apply information if you do not teach them how to do so. We have all known professors like the psychology instructor who limits her lectures to presenting facts and figures and then asks students to develop their own theory of personality on the final exam.

Similarly, if you are teaching students how to analyze new situations, you should not be limiting your test questions to recall and recognition items. You use test scores to make interpretations about how much of the course material your students have mastered. Obviously, you want these inferences to be valid to the extent possible. The validity of the inferences made from classroom test scores primarily rests on the validation of the content of the test. Interpretations about achievement based on the test scores are likely to be appropriate when your test items are a representative sample of the course content and objectives.

It is seldom appropriate, especially in introductory courses, to expect much learning (and teaching) beyond the application level. We are not suggesting that you attempt to teach and test at all six levels of the taxonomy. We are recommending that you use the taxonomy to match targeted levels of teaching, learning, and testing. The following are some examples of instructional objectives and matching test items that are written at each of the six taxonomic levels. For each, the level of desired behavior expressed in the objective must be acquired for students to answer the corresponding test item correctly.

Knowledge Level

Objective. The student will be able to identify various kinds of schizophrenia.

Test Item. Which of the following is NOT a type of schizophrenia?
    a. Hebephrenic
    b. Catatonic
    c. Paranoid
    d. Autistic

Comprehension Level

Objective. The student will be able to provide examples of several psychological concepts.

Test Item. Which of the following would be an instance of compliance?

a. Moving away from the group norm regardless of prior opinions.
b. Maintaining one's belief in the face of group pressure to change those beliefs.
c. Following group norms in overt behavior but not cognitively.
d. Seeking group consensus without carefully considering all possible arguments.

Application Level

Objective. The student will be able to calculate the arithmetic mean for a given set of numbers.

Test Item.

10	3
8	2
7	4
5	1

The arithmetic mean for the above set of numbers is
a. 8
b. 7
c. 6
d. 5

Analysis Level

Objective. The student will be able to analyze given economic situations by citing possible reasons for their existence.

Test Item. Which of the following conditions would most likely contribute to a state of high inflation?
a. High growth rate and low unemployment
b. Higher taxes and high unemployment
c. Low growth rate and low unemployment
d. Lower taxes and high unemployment

Synthesis Level

Objective. Given a set of research findings, the student will be able to make generalizations about the research results.

Test Item. Deutsch has carried out a number of experiments on the bargaining process. Generalizing from his results, we can conclude that:
    a. The more threatening the weapons that bargainers acquire, the more likely they are to compete.
    b. The more threatening the weapons that bargainers have, the more likely they are to cooperate.
    c. Threatening weapons do not influence bargaining as much as saving face does.
    d. We cannot accurately conclude any of the above.

Evaluation Level

Objective. The student can recognize the values and points of view used in a particular judgment of a work.

Test Item. Which of the following best interprets and clarifies the statement: "Geology for the most part is an observational science rather than an experimental science"?
    a. The phenomena of geology are usually too vast in time and scale for investigation under controlled conditions.
    b. It is impossible to investigate geological phenomena in the laboratory.
    c. An open mind can be better retained by observing nature as it is than as it performs under artificial conditions.
    d. As long as geological processes are easily visible, it is unnecessary to carry out experiments.

The taxonomic level of a test item is not always apparent without first knowing how the material was presented to the students. For example, the synthesis-level example item may only be written at the knowledge level if you discuss these alternative conclusions in class.

Activity: Think about your teaching and consider at what levels of the taxonomy you are teaching. Now, take one of your old exams and classify each item into one of the six levels of the taxonomy. Does your testing correspond to your teaching? For many instructors it does not. Often instructors are asking too much or too little of their students at testing time. The next time you need to prepare an exam, before you write a single test item, take a few minutes to consider what type of behaviors you expect from your students.

Developing a Testing Blueprint

A common complaint about instructors that appears on many student evaluation forms is their failure to test the important content. How many times have students complained, "For hours I studied material that was hardly covered on the exam!" or "I didn't know that was going to be on the exam!" One way to minimize these complaints (and possible real occurrences) is to combine content headings and course objectives to make a testing blueprint or a table of specifications.

As with instructional objectives, tables of specifications can be simple or complicated to construct. We choose the simple method.

Activity: Take a piece of paper and make a grid of boxes placed in columns and rows. Take your major content headings from your lectures and text and use them to label the rows. Review the objectives that you have noted for each lecture and classify them into major behavioral categories (e.g., knowledge of basic facts and ability to apply concepts and rules). These behavioral categories are used to label your columns on the grid.

To illustrate this activity, we show in Table 1.1 specifications for a test on theories and systems of psychology. The column headings are expected student outcomes and the row headings are theories and systems of psychology.

Table 1.1 Specifications for a 60-Item Test on Theories and Systems of Psychology

| Content Areas | Instructional Objectives | | | | Total Items |
	Knows Basic Antecedents	Knows Founding Psychologists	Knows Basic Tenets	Can Compare and Contrast Systems	
Structuralism	2	2	2	2	8
Functionalism	2	2	2	2	8
Modern Association	2	2	3	3	10
Behaviorism	2	3	3	4	12
Gestalt	3	2	3	2	10
Existential Psychology	3	3	3	3	12
Total Items	14	14	16	16	60

Developing a classroom exam means filling in the table with test items. After an item is written that covers knowledge of the founding psychologists of behaviorism, a test item number (the item's number on the exam) can be placed in the fourth row, second column box. By writing items and completing the entire grid with test item numbers you develop a test that tests what you said you were going to test at your desired level of learning. Without the grid, instructors often leave several boxes empty and untested because they forget to cover such material or they find it difficult to write items covering those objectives. We can also differentially weight objective/content areas by including more items in particular boxes. Completion of the grid should minimize student complaints that you failed to test the important material.

Activity: To see how well you do in covering targeted objective/ content areas, take an old exam and try to build a table of specifications. How well did you cover the desired content?

What is the next testing or grading activity? You have determined what to test by developing course objectives and test specifications. The next activity is to develop a testing plan to determine *how* to test. Chapter 2 provides suggestions for establishing a testing plan.

2 | Developing a Test Plan

A testing plan needs to be developed before writing the first test item. You can begin to develop your testing plan by answering the following questions:

- What is the purpose of the exam?
- How difficult should you make the test?
- Who is taking the exam?
- How many students are taking the test?
- How much time has been provided for testing?
- How many exams are scheduled?
- What type of test (multiple choice, essay, true-false, etc.) is desirable?

What Is the Purpose of the Exam?

Is the intent of the test diagnostic, to help both you and your students learn of particular problem areas? Or is the purpose to test students for the assignment of course grades? The evaluation field refers to these two purposes as *formative* and *summative*, respectively. Formative exams are not used for making pass-fail decisions, as summative exams are, but rather for identifying areas of student weakness that may be remediated by the instructor. Formative exams can be ungraded quizzes that are periodically administered to learn of student or instructor weaknesses. Summative exams are midterms and finals, given at the end of a unit to be used for assigning grades.

The difficulty level and discriminating power (i.e., ability to identify students of different ability levels) of a classroom exam are guided by the purpose of the testing. Testing for the assignment of grades requires items at different levels of difficulty so as to identify students with different levels of knowledge. Formative exams present items that inform you of student problems with the content or its presentation. These items may be easy checks of mastery to see that all students have the prerequisite knowledge to move on to more difficult material or items that present difficult challenges to assess the upper levels of student understanding. How often do you quiz students to determine their level of understanding?

Activity: Administer a short quiz to your students that covers content covered so far in class. How well did you and your class do? Are there areas that need reteaching?

If the classroom exam is to be used summatively for the assignment of course grades, are you more concerned about judging student quality by comparing the performances of the students with one another or by assessing student achievement of course objectives? *Norm-referenced* testing is used to assign grades on the basis of comparing student performance, whereas *criterion-referenced* testing is used to assign grades on the accomplishment of course objectives, regardless of class ranking. Stated differently, there is a limited number of A's awarded with a norm-referenced test, whereas all students can receive an A on a criterion-referenced test. Once again, the difficulty level and discriminating power of an exam is guided by the decision to use a norm- or criterion-referenced approach to testing. Norm-referenced tests require items at different difficulty levels so as to discriminate among students and avoid awarding only one or two grades.

Criterion-referenced tests usually are better diagnostic measures than are norm-referenced exams. Criterion-referenced testing is useful when it is necessary to determine whether students have acquired the necessary knowledge to move on to the next level of difficulty. To illustrate, we have both taught our department's introductory statistics class. Typically, the course is composed of undergraduate students, beginning graduate students, and some advanced doctoral students reviewing for qualifying exams. Because of the diversity of student ability, motivation, and background we do not believe that it would be fair to make (norm-referenced) student comparisons. On the first day of class we describe to the students the diversity of the group (if they didn't already notice it!) but explain how everyone in the class can receive an *A*. We tell the students not to worry about the performance of their advanced classmates but to demonstrate their learning on the exams.

How Difficult Should You Make the Test?

As previously stated, the intent of a criterion-referenced test is to determine what students know rather than how much more they know than someone else. All students should perceive the test as easy if they know the material. This is not the case if a norm-reference model is used. To identify students at different levels of knowledge some items need to be more difficult than others. How difficult? The test items should be sufficiently difficult to allow you to meet your testing needs, whether it is to identify students with and without minimal competency or to assign grades of *A, B, C, D,* and *F.*

One way to include items at a desired difficulty level is to maintain records of test item statistics. (Item statistics will be covered in a later chapter, but for now we can think of them as indicators of the difficulty and discriminating ability of an item.) How easy or difficult were the items when used in the past? We can review the statistics for old items or estimate new statistics for similar but new items. Another way to make a test more difficult and discriminating is to include questions that go beyond what has been memorized and ask students to apply their knowledge to new situations or problems. We have found that tests that only cover material that has been specifically taught in class are apt to have scores that bunch near the top of the range. These tests will be of little help in determining an accurate rank order of achievement. However, we do not recommend testing inconsequential details just to separate students. Instead, focus on important understandings that you believe the better students should have—the kind of understandings that you would not expect of less competent students.

Activity: Review one of your old tests and see if you included material taught in and out of class. Did you mean to include one or the other or both? How difficult were the items covering material taught in class compared with items covering material learned outside the classroom?

Who Is Taking the Exam?

The student population may affect your testing decisions. If you are teaching an introductory course to students with no content expertise you may want to test (and teach) at the lower levels of the taxonomy. You may also want to administer several short quizzes or tests to increase your opportunities to provide useful feedback to these novice students. You may want to challenge experienced seniors or honor students by testing at the upper levels of the taxonomy. If you are teaching a course to students with diverse abilities, backgrounds, and motivations for taking the course you may not want to make student comparisons by using a norm-referenced testing approach. You may instead select a criterion-referenced approach, which does not rely on student comparisons.

How Many Students Are in the Course?

The number of students in class may affect your selection of testing formats or the number of testing situations. Although essay tests are easier to construct than multiple-choice exams, essays can be quite time-consuming and difficult to grade for large classes. The question you face with large classes is whether you are willing to put your time in up front in developing multiple-choice items or at the end of the course by grading stacks of essay exams.

Objective exams, such as multiple-choice tests, can be administered with answer sheets that can be quickly scored by hand or scored and analyzed by machine. Many college campuses have optical scanners that convert answer-sheet data to computer disk to be analyzed on a computer. Some campuses are fortunate to have a testing office that will do the analysis for you.

What Is the Testing Schedule?

How many hours are you allocating for classroom testing? There are several advantages to having more rather than less testing. Administering more short exams and fewer long exams provides more coverage of course content. Frequent testing minimizes lengthy periods between exams, thus reducing memory decay. Frequent testing also provides more opportunities for feedback to and from the students. Low-achieving students can be informed well before the midterm that they need to try harder or to receive additional help. Furthermore, final course grades increase in accuracy when the number of graded components (i.e., exams, papers, projects) is high. Everyone will have an off day and a poor test performance. More rather than fewer tests account for these off performances, placing less weight on any one exam score.

The testing schedule may also affect the type of exam administered. For example, if final exam day is 2 days before grades are to be posted, a professor may prefer to score 100 multiple-choice exams quickly rather than take hours to read 100 essay papers. Multiple-choice items generally take more time to prepare than do essay items, but the former can be graded in much less time.

How Many Items Should You Have on Your Tests?

Instructors are always asking us how many items to include on an exam. Obviously the answer depends on the complexity of the content, the format of the items, and the ability level of the students. It is our opinion that all students in the class should be given sufficient time to complete the test. We believe that, in general, it is more important to measure what students know rather than how fast they can demonstrate their knowledge. We realize that some compulsive and anxious students will take as much time as is provided. However, an effort should be made to see that all your students can complete the exam in the time period provided. Past experience with similar tests and students can be your best guide for determining the number of items.

A useful rule of thumb for selecting an appropriate number of test items is to take the test yourself and then triple the amount of time that you spend to estimate required student time.

Other considerations for choosing an appropriate number of items is the number of course objectives to be covered by the exam and the type of exam question used. Testing experts recommend covering each objective with more than one test item. You may have insufficient testing time if you are trying to test too much with each exam. Usually in these cases we often recommend adding more tests to cover important objectives or combining/reducing objectives. Remember that more content can be covered with objective tests (multiple choice or true-false) than with essay or short-answer tests;

50-minute essay exams cannot cover the same number of objectives as can 50-minute multiple-choice exams.

What Type of Classroom Exam Question Is Desirable?

There are two general categories of test items on most classroom exams: objective items (e.g., multiple choice, true-false, and matching), which require students to select the correct response from several alternatives or to supply a word or short phrase to answer a question or complete a statement, and constructed response items (e.g., short answer/completion, essays, and problem solving), which require students to organize and present an original answer. There are advantages and disadvantages for using the different item types.

Activity: To begin our discussion of the relative merits of different types of test items, test your knowledge of objective and essay (including problem solving) questions by answering the following seven questions:

Test Item Quiz

	Circle the correct response		
1. Essay exams are easier to construct than objective items.	T	F	?
2. Essay exams require more thorough student preparation and study time than objective items.	T	F	?
3. Essay exams require writing skills, whereas objective exams do not.	T	F	?
4. Essay exams teach a person how to write.	T	F	?
5. Objective exams encourage more guessing than essay exams.	T	F	?

6. Essay exams limit the extent of   T   F   ?
   content covered.
7. Essay and objective exams can   T   F   ?
   be used to measure the same
   content and abilities.

Quiz Answers

1. TRUE   Essay items are generally easier and less time-consuming to construct than are objective test items. Technically correct and content-appropriate multiple-choice and true-false items require an extensive amount of time to write and revise. For example, a professional item writer produces only 9 to 10 usable multiple-choice items a day.

2. UNDECIDED   According to research findings it is still undetermined whether or not essay tests require or facilitate more thorough (or even different) student understanding.

3. TRUE   Writing skills do affect a student's ability to communicate the correct factual information through an essay response. Consequently, students with good writing skills have an advantage over students who have difficulty expressing themselves through writing.

4. FALSE   Essays cannot teach a student how to write, but they can be used to emphasize the importance of being able to communicate through writing. Consistent use of essay exams may encourage the knowledgeable but poor-writing student to improve his or her writing to improve test performance.

5. UNDECIDED   Both item types encourage some form of guessing. Multiple-choice, true-false, and

matching items can be correctly answered through guessing, yet essay questions can be responded to through well-written bluffing.

6. TRUE   Because of the extent of time required by the student to respond to an essay question, only a few essay questions can be included on a classroom exam. A larger number of objective items can be tested in the same amount of time, thus enabling the objective tests to cover more content than essay exams.

7. TRUE   Both item types can measure similar content or learning objectives. Research has shown that students respond almost identically to essay and objective test items covering the same content. Hogan's (1981) review of research comparing essay and objective test performances reached the same conclusion made by Patterson (1926): "There seems to be no escape from the conclusions that the two types of exams are measuring identical things" (p. 246). This conclusion should not be surprising. A well-written essay question requires students (1) to have a store of knowledge, (2) to be able to relate facts and principles, and (3) to be able to organize such information into a coherent and logical written expression, whereas an objective test item requires students (1) to have a store of knowledge, (2) to be able to relate facts and principles, and (3) to be able to organize such information into a coherent and logical choice among several alternatives.

Answers to the quiz demonstrate that both types of test items can be used to measure almost any important educational achievement, whether it is testing the ability to think critically or to solve problems. There are situations, however, when one type of item is preferable. Objective tests are more appropriate when testing large classes, when highly reliable scores must be obtained as efficiently and as quickly as possible, or when absolute objectivity and freedom from scorer bias are essential. Essay exams are favored when you wish to encourage the development of writing skills and to assess the student's ability to create and organize an original response. Essays are also preferred by instructors who have more confidence in their ability to grade essay responses equitably than their ability to write good objective test items. Furthermore, certain learning objectives may be more appropriately measured by an essay question than by an objective item and vice versa. For example, an essay question may be the more appropriate method for measuring a learning objective that asks students to appraise and critique a written passage, whereas objective items may be better suited for testing objectives requiring students to identify parts of the human skeleton.

Whenever possible, we recommend including both objective and constructed-response items on a classroom exam. Students have different learning styles and test-taking abilities; some are better essay writers than choosers of multiple-choice alternatives. By using different types of exam items, you can accommodate individual differences and allow each student an opportunity to test in a way that maximizes his or her performance.

Activity: Analyze your testing situation by considering your skills as a test writer, your learning objectives, your purpose(s) for testing, and any conditional constraints such as time available for testing and grading. Are you better served by essay or objectives items or both?

What is the next testing or grading activity? You have selected your test content and developed a testing plan that identified the type of tests you want to develop and administer. The next activity is to develop test items or select items from existing sources. Chapter 3 provides guidelines for writing and judging the quality of different types of test items.

3 | Suggestions for Writing Objective Test Items

The following types of objective test items are discussed in this chapter:

- Multiple Choice
- True-False
- Matching
- Additional Item Types

Multiple-Choice Test Items

Two types of multiple-choice items are described in this section: multiple choice and complex multiple choice. The multiple-choice item consists of two parts: the *stem*, which identifies the question or problem, and the *response alternatives*. Students are asked to select the one alternative that best completes the statement or answers the question. Here's an example of a multiple-choice item:

Item Stem: The psychodynamic perspective originated in the theory of

Response Alternatives:
    a. Freud.
    b. Szasz.
    c. Horney.
    d. Jung.

A complex multiple-choice item includes three parts: a stem, four or five statements, and four or five response alternatives consisting of combinations of the presented statements. Students are asked to select the alternative that presents the best combination of statements that answers the question presented in the stem. Here's an example:

Item Stem: Which of the following behaviors represents a late maturation or a minor deviation from the normal pattern of development?

Statements:
    1. 4-month-old baby cannot hold up head.
    2. 2-year-old boy does not walk alone.
    3. 13-year-old boy has not yet reached puberty.
    4. 4-year-old girl has spoken vocabulary of 150 words.

Alternatives:
    a. 1, 2, and 3.
    b. 1, 3.
    c. 2, 3, and 4.
    d. 2 and 4.
    e. all of the above.

Advantages of Using Multiple-Choice Items

Multiple-choice items can provide . . .

➜ versatility in measuring all levels of cognitive ability,
➜ highly reliable test scores,
➜ scoring efficiency and accuracy,
➜ objective measurement of student achievement or ability,
➜ a wide sampling of content or objectives,
➜ a reduced guessing factor compared with true-false items, and
➜ different response alternatives that can provide diagnostic feedback.

Limitations of Using Multiple-Choice Items

Multiple-choice items . . .

➜ are difficult and time-consuming to construct,
➜ lead an instructor to favor simple recall of facts,
➜ place a high degree of dependence on the student's reading ability and instructor's writing ability, and
➜ are particularly subject to clueing. (Students can often deduce the correct response by elimination.)

Suggestions for Using Multiple-Choice Items

The Stem

Avoid statements that fail to present a complete thought or question.

Schizophrenia
   a. is caused by excessive role playing in childhood.
   b. causes hallucinations.
   c. is a tendency toward ritualistic behavior.
   d. is a psychosocial disorder.

Better:

Schizophrenia is described as
   a. an alternation between two or more personalities.

b. a tendency toward ritualistic behavior.
c. a fragmentation of psychological functioning.
d. an inability to inhibit emotional outbursts.

What is being tested about schizophrenia in the example item? Is the student expected to know causes of schizophrenia, symptoms of schizophrenia, or descriptions of schizophrenia? As written, the item is not a multiple-choice item but rather four separate true-false items. The instructor may as well have written four true-false items worth one point each. In multiple-choice items, the stem should identify a problem so the student can read a set of parallel constructed alternatives with a clear purpose in mind. After reading the stem students should be capable of searching their memory for the correct answer even before reading the response alternatives. The improved item stem instructs students to select a description of schizophrenia from among the alternatives.

Avoid stems that ask for a series of multiple true-false responses.

Which of the following is true about the middle adult years?
  a. It encompasses ages 19 to 30.
  b. It is the most conflict-free period of life.
  c. It is characterized by dramatic changes in our sense of values.
  d. It is marked by a conflict between intimacy and isolation.

Better:

According to Erickson, the middle adult years are characterized by the conflict between _____ and _____ .
  a. intimacy; isolation
  b. generativity; stagnation
  c. integrity; despair
  d. industry; despondency

The instructor fails to identify the intended problem or question in the example item stem. The student must respond to each alternative as an independent true-false item. The improved item poses a question regarding Erickson's belief about the conflicts experienced in the middle adult years.

Eliminate excessive wording and irrelevant information.

Sheldon developed a highly controversial theory of personality based on body type and temperament of the individual. Which of the following is a criticism of Sheldon's work?
   a. He was influenced too much by Freudian psychoanalysis.
   b. His ratings of physique and temperament were not independent.
   c. He failed to use an empirical approach.
   d. His research sample was improperly selected.

Better:

Which of the following is a criticism of Sheldon's theory of personality?

The first sentence in the example item stem describing Sheldon's work is referred to as an *instructional aside*. Instructional asides present information that should already be known by the student. Students who need to be taught about Sheldon's theory in the stem of an item are unable to answer many questions about the theory. At testing time it is appropriate to test content, not to attempt to teach content. In this example, if the instructor wants to avoid teaching content but help prompt memory he or she could include in the stem reference to Sheldon's work with personality theory. Instructional asides should not be confused with additional comments aimed at describing a situation or setting a context, for example, phrases such as these: "According to the information-processing approach" and "Because exercise and stress produce very similar physiological reactions."

Include in the stem any word(s) that might otherwise be repeated in each alternative.

The receptors for the vestibular sense are located
    a. in the fovea.
    b. in the brain.
    c. in the middle ear.
    d. in the inner ear.

Better:

The receptors for the vestibular senses are located in the

You can reduce reading time and the student's chance of missing key words embedded in an alternative by minimizing the length of the alternatives.

Use negatively stated stems sparingly. When used, underline and/or capitalize the negative word.

Which is not a major technique for studying brain function?
    a. Accident and injury
    b. Cutting and removing
    c. Electrical stimulation
    d. Direct phrenology

Better:

Which is NOT a major technique for studying brain function?

For certain content we seem to find it much easier to write an item using a negatively worded stem. There is nothing wrong or inappropriate with this procedure; however, we can improve item and student performance by using these items sparingly and by highlighting the negative qualifier. Our intent should be to measure what students have learned while helping them to avoid common testing mistakes such as misreading items.

When using incomplete statements avoid beginning with the blank space.

_____ is the *least* severe form of behavior disorder.
 a. Psychosis
 b. Panic disorder
 c. Neurasthenia
 d. Neurosis

Better:

The *least* severe form of behavior disorder is _____ .

The intent of the question is more evident if the blank space is provided at the end of the stem. Blanks at the beginning of the stem commonly result in students reading and rereading the item to understand better the intent of the question (which is an inefficient use of testing time).

Use familiar language.

According to Freud the raison d'être for hysteria was
 a. sexual conflicts.
 b. unresolved feelings of guilt.
 c. latent tendencies.
 d. repressed fear.

Better:

According to Freud hysteria was caused by

Sometimes what appears to be a clever and creative item to the instructor is an unnecessary source of confusion to the student. This example item was actually taken from a textbook item bank. We doubt that this item could be administered without at least one student in an introductory psychology class asking for clarification. It is not always obvious what is difficult vocabulary, unfamiliar language, or unknown situations. We should not assume that references to campus sports, television programs, or popular sayings are common knowledge for all students. In addition to student confusion, unfamiliar references or terminology also introduces a source of irrelevant difficulty, increasing the difficulty of some items for reasons unrelated to test content.

Provide sufficient information in the stem to allow students to respond to the question.

How many interrelated stages to creative problem solving are there?
   a. Three
   b. Four
   c. Seven
   d. Ten

Better:

The *textbook* indicates that there are _____ interrelated stages to creative problem solving.

In most content areas there are conflicting perspectives or theories. It is important to provide sufficient direction in the stem to enable students to understand the referent or context of the item. This may mean referencing the textbook, the lectures, or a particular individual in the question.

The Item Alternatives

Make sure there is one correct or best response.

Which of the following does not belong with the others?

a. Wundt
b. Structuralism
c. James
d. Titchener

There are two correct responses to the example item. Both
b and *c* are correct responses but for two different reasons. The
item was written to separate James (*c*) from the school of structuralism and the two structuralist psychologists. However, a
clever student could make a case that alternative *b* is correct
because it is the name of a school of psychology and not the
name of a psychologist as are the other three alternatives. It
is desirable to catch multiple correct answers before your
students do (and they always do!).

**Make all alternatives plausible and equally attractive to both
less-knowledgeable and skillful students.**

The concept of the inferiority complex was contributed by
   a. Adler.
   b. Freud.
   c. Jung.
   d. Lincoln.

Better:
   a. Adler.
   b. Freud.
   c. Jung.
   d. Horney.

Or:

The number of photoreceptors in the retina of each human
eye is about
   a. 100,000.
   b. 2 million.
   c. 115 million.
   d. 2.37 billion.

Better:
  a. 5 million.
  b. 35 million.
  c. 65 million.
  d. 115 million.

The multiple-choice format was developed to reduce the guessing factor of true-false items. However, to do so each of the alternatives must be equally attractive to the less-able student. In the first example, Lincoln should conspicuously stand out from the names of famous psychologists. In the second example the less-able student need only remember reading the word *million* to be able to eliminate alternatives *a* and *d*. The improved second item should be more difficult and challenging because of the similarity of alternatives.

Minimize the use of the *all-of-the-above* and *none-of-the-above* alternatives.

Problem representation involves
  a. determining which factors matter and which do not.
  b. the initial state of problem solving.
  c. both a and b.
  d. neither a nor b.

Better:
  a. determining which factors matter and which do not.
  b. the initial state of problem solving.
  c. reducing the problem to manageable segments.
  d. all of the above.

Too often instructors use none-of-the-above and all-of-the-above alternatives when they are unable to create a good fourth alternative. Students learn quickly to eliminate these alternatives and reduce the guessing factor from one out of four to one out of three. If these alternatives are used they should appear early in the exam as the correct answer to cue students that these alternatives should be taken seriously. We do not recommend including both the none-of-the-above and all-of-the-above alternatives in the same item, as done in the example item. Instead, you could create a new alternative as illustrated or rewrite the item as a true-false item.

Use between three and five alternatives for each item.

What function is performed by the sensory neurons?
  a. Receive information from the environment.
  b. Carry information from the central nervous system to the muscles.
  c. Connect one neuron to another.
  d. Are only found inside the brain.

Better:
  a. Receive information from the environment.
  b. Carry information from the central nervous system to the muscles.
  c. Connect one neuron to another.

It is not easy to develop one correct response and three or four appealing distracters. Often our third incorrect alternative is so obviously wrong that it is quickly discarded by the students. Despite reducing the guessing factor compared with four- or five-choice multiple-choice items, three-choice items enable the instructor to avoid poorly written fourth alternatives, reduce reading time, and cover more content by adding more shorter items to the test. Items with more than five responses add significantly to the reading time of the student, are more difficult to write, and can add unnecessary confusion to question.

> *A Helpful Suggestion:* You will have better quality distracters if you try to write one more distracter than you plan to use and then select the best.

All alternatives should be approximately equal in length.

Latane and Darley's smoke-filled room experiment suggested that people are less likely to help in groups than alone, because people
   a. in groups talk to one another.
   b. who are alone are more attentive.
   c. in groups do not display pluralistic ignorance.
   d. in groups allow others to define the situation as a non-emergency.

Better:

Latane and Darley's smoke-filled room experiment suggested that people are less likely to help in groups than alone, because people in groups
   a. talk to one another.
   b. are less attentive than people who are alone.
   c. do not display pluralistic ignorance.
   d. allow others to define nonemergencies.

In trying to make the correct alternative unquestionably correct, we often make it longer than the distracters by adding qualifiers and clauses. The best example of this came to our attention from a professor in history. After reviewing one of his classroom exams we noted how he had a disproportionately high number of *c* and *d* response alternatives as the correct answer. He was unaware of the situation and explained how he had typed his exam. For each item he placed the smallest alternative in the *a* position, the second smallest alternative in the *b* position, the second longest alternative in the *c* position, and the longest alternative in the *d* position. Thus the longest responses (*c* and *d*) were most often the correct responses! To avoid cuing the students to the correct response, make all of the alternatives approximately equal in length.

Make alternatives parallel in construction and consistent with the stem.

Which of the following is NOT a defense mechanism?
a. Conflict
b. Repression
c. Reaction formation
d. Rationalization

Better:
a. Rationalization
b Repression
c. Reaction formation
d. Regression

Alternative *a* in the first example is different from the other alternatives, because it is the only one that doesn't begin with the letter *r*. Test-wise students may believe that the correct response must begin with the letter *r*, because the instructor is trying fool them with two other words beginning with *r*, thus they eliminate the first alternative and increase their chances for answering correctly. To avoid giving the advantage to test-wise students, alternatives should be parallel in construction and, therefore, equally attractive to the students.

When possible, present alternatives in some logical order (e.g., most to least and chronological).

In the course of dark adaptation, the eye's best sensitivity to wavelength shifts to
a. 580 millimicrons.
b. 477 millimicrons.
c. 505 millimicrons.
d. 600 millimicrons.

Better:
a. 600 millimicrons.
b. 580 millimicrons.

c. 505 millimicrons.
d. 477 millimicrons.

This is a small point but one that can possibly help students avoid careless errors. If students know the correct answer before looking at the alternatives their task in selecting the correct response is made easier and faster by arranging the alternatives in some logical order.

Make the alternatives mutually exclusive.

Rods are found in the
  a. blind spot.
  b. fovea.
  c. periphery of the retina.
  d. back of the eye.

Better:
  a. blind spot.
  b. periphery of the fovea.
  c. periphery of the retina.
  d. cornea.

Unless otherwise indicated there should be only one correct response to a multiple-choice item. In the example item, rods are located in the periphery of the retina, which is located in the back of the eye. Therefore, both alternatives *c* and *d* are correct.

Avoid overly wordy alternatives that become confusing and difficult to read.

Flooding differs from systematic desensitization in that
  a. the former is based on classical conditioning and the latter on operant conditioning.
  b. systematic desensitization requires insight and the flooding does not.

    c. flooding has you start at the top of your fear hierarchy and systematic desensitization has you start at the bottom and work up gradually.

    d. flooding emphasizes the use of cognitions to a much greater extent than does systematic desensitization.

Better:

Flooding differs from systematic desensitization in that flooding
    a. is based on classical rather than operant conditioning.
    b. doesn't require insight.
    c. starts at the top of the fear hierarchy.
    d. places greater emphasis on the use of cognitions.

The appearance of the two example items should demonstrate why it is important to reduce unnecessary words from the alternatives. The first looks long and confusing, whereas the second does not. You can minimize reading errors and lessen response time by reducing the wordiness of an item.

Avoid irrelevant cues such as grammatical structure, well-known word associations, or connections between the stem and the correct answer.

School psychologists who examine and place children in special education settings often apply the research done by
    a. biopsychologists.
    b. educational psychologists.
    c. clinical psychologists.
    d. counseling psychologists.

Better:

School psychologists often apply the research done by

Or:

Nodes of Ranvier are located on a
   a. dendrite.
   b. axon.
   c. soma.
   d. axon button.

Better:

Nodes of Ranvier are located on
   a. a dendrite.
   b. an axon.
   c. a soma.
   d. an axon button.

Or:

The two branches of the autonomic nervous system are
   a. sympathetic and epinephrine.
   b. parasympathetic and sympathetic.
   c. visceral and parasympathetic.
   d. thyrotropic and sympathetic.

Better:

What are the two branches of the autonomic nervous system?

_____ and _____   (fill in the blanks)

Each of the examples demonstrate clues that test-wise students can find to increase their chances of correctly answering the question. The first example uses the word *education* in the stem and the correct alternative. The second example provides a grammatical clue that can be used to eliminate two of the distracters. The final example provides a correct alternative that will just sound right to the test-wise student. Because of the sound-alike nature of the words *sympathetic* and *parasympathetic*, the multiple-choice format may not be as suitable as the fill-in-the-blank format to test this content. Students lacking in test-taking ability will not be placed at a disadvantage with well-written items that do not provide clues to the correct response.

Avoid language that may offend or exclude a particular group of individuals.

If a person sustained brain damage to his medulla, he may have trouble
  a. seeing.
  b. talking.
  c. living.
  d. balancing.

Better:

Individuals sustaining brain damage to the medulla have most trouble

Or:

Research has found that psychiatrists often neglect their wives and children.
  a. True
  b. False

Better:

Research has found that psychiatrists often neglect their families.

Or:

Which of the following is a characteristic of persons with Down's syndrome?

    a. Larger than normal head
    b. Obesity
    c. Oriental-like skin folds over the eyes
    d. Above average height

Better:
    a. Larger than normal head
    b. Obesity
    c. Downward sloping skin fold over the eyes
    d. Above average height

Or:

Congress gave African-Americans broad enforcement and protection of their right to vote in 1964.
    a. True
    b. False

Better:

African-Americans won broad enforcement and protection of their rights to vote in 1964.

In most cases the easiest way to handle issues of gender language, as demonstrated in the first example item, is to use plural wording. But gender or racial issues in item development extend beyond the inappropriate use of *he* and *she*. You should refrain from writing items that (a) stereotype members of a group, (b) offend individuals with inappropriate references to race or culture, and (c) wrongly depict relations of status and power. The second example item presents a stereotype that all psychiatrists are male. In the third example item, a physical characteristic seen in Down's syndrome doesn't need to be associated with a physical characteristic associated with Asians. The fourth example misleads the student to believe that African-Americans did nothing to gain the right to vote. Other examples of stereotyping and offensive language are presented by the National Evaluation Systems (1987) and the Educational Testing Service (1987).

Randomly distribute the correct response among the alternative positions throughout the test, having approximately the same proportion of *a*'s, *b*'s, *c*'s, *d*'s, and *e*'s as the correct response.

Activity: The next time you write multiple-choice items use the following checklist to determine which suggestions you followed.

_____ When possible, I stated the stem as a direct question rather than as an incomplete statement.

_____ I presented a definite, explicit, and singular question or problem in the stem.

_____ I eliminated excessive verbiage or irrelevant information from the stem.

_____ I included in the stem any word(s) that might have otherwise been repeated in each alternative.

_____ I used negatively stated stems sparingly. When used, I underlined and/or capitalized the negative word(s).

_____ I made all alternatives plausible and attractive to the less-knowledgeable student as well as the skillful student.

_____ I made the alternatives grammatically parallel with each other and consistent with the stem.

_____ I made the alternatives mutually exclusive.

_____ When possible, I presented alternatives in some logical order (e.g., chronologically and most to least).

_____ I made sure there was only one correct or best response per item.

_____ I made the alternatives approximately equal in length.

_____ I avoided irrelevant clues such as grammatical structure, well-known verbal associations, or connections between stem and answer.

_____ I used at least three alternatives for each item.

_____ I randomly distributed the correct response among the alternative positions throughout the test and gave each alternative position approximately the same number of correct responses.

_____ I used the alternatives *none of the above* and *all of the above* sparingly. When used, such alternatives were occasionally the correct response.

_____ I avoided language that may offend or exclude a particular group of individuals.

True-False Test Items

A true-false item can be written in one of four forms: simple, complex, compound, or multiple. Answers can consist of only two choices (simple), more than two choices (complex), or two choices plus a conditional completion response (compound). The complex form resembles a multiple-choice item in appearance, however, rather than selecting one best answer from several alternatives, examinees respond to each of the several alternatives as separate true-false statements. Here's an example of a simple true-false item:

The acquisition of morality
is a developmental process.   True   False

This is a complex true-false item:

The acquisition of morality
is a developmental process.   True   False   Opinion

A compound true-false item looks like this:

The acquisition of morality is   True   False
a developmental process.
If this statement is false,
what makes it false?   _____

                               _____

An example of a multiple true-false item is the following:

Which of the following conclusions about Milgram's research on obedience is true? (Indicate True or False on the line)

_____ 1. Our tendency to obey the commands of authority figures is strong.

_____ 2. Obedience is increased when the "victim" is more distant.

_____ 3. Obedience is reduced if the subject believes he or she is fully responsible for the outcome.

Advantages of Using True-False Items

True-false items can provide . . .

→ the widest sampling of content or objectives per unit of testing time,

→ scoring efficiency and accuracy,

→ versatility in measuring all levels of cognitive ability,

→ highly reliable test scores, and

→ an objective measurement of student achievement or ability.

Limitations of Using True-False Items

True-false items . . .

→ incorporate an extremely high guessing factor. For simple true-false items, each student has a 50-50 chance of correctly answering the item without any knowledge of the item's content,

→ can often lead an instructor to write ambiguous statements because of the difficulty of writing statements that are unequivocally true or false,

→ do not discriminate between students of varying ability as well as other item types do,

→ can often include more irrelevant clues than do other item types, and

→ can often lead an instructor to favor testing of trivial knowledge.

Suggestions for Using True-False Items

Test important content and avoid trivial statements.

Philosophy and physiology are ancient fields of study.

Better:

Psychology is a hybrid science combining components of both philosophy and physiology.

The important content is the relationship between psychology, physiology, and philosophy, not some simple statement found in the text that stresses the age of philosophy and physiology. Besides, who could disagree with the first statement? True-false items are often maligned for testing trivial, low-level material. However, this criticism should be made of the test writer, not of the test format. True-false items can be written to test knowledge at all levels of learning. Ebel (1972, pp. 183-184) provides some excellent examples of true-false items written at different levels of learning:

Factual. The standard deviation of an ideal set of stanine scores is 5.

Relational. The larger the number of scores in a set, the larger the standard deviation.

Predictive. One could expect to increase the reliability coefficient of a test from 0.30 to 0.60 by doubling the number of test items.

Procedural. To determine the range of a set of scores one must know the number of scores in the set.

Evaluative. It is difficult to obtain reliable scores from a group in which the range of abilities is very wide.

Avoid lifting statements from books or lectures that can be answered by simple memorization.

Psychology is the scientific study of behavior and mental processes.

Independent variables are manipulated by the experimenter.

Social psychology is the study of social interaction.

All three examples were either written in the text or stated in the lecture and can be answered correctly by simple memorization. Such content is often better left untested.

Provide sufficient information in the statement to allow students to respond correctly.

Gender roles are developed by the process of identification with one parent.

Better:

According to the psychoanalytic perspective, gender roles are developed by the process of identification with one parent.

With some content, the truth of a statement may rest in knowing its context, that is, who said it, how was it stated, why was it said, and so on.

Express a single idea in each statement.

The mean, median, and mode are measures of central tendency, whereas the standard deviation and range are measures of variability.

Better:

The mean and standard deviation are measures of central tendency.

Try not to test too much content or too many ideas in a single item. One of the purposes of testing is to help determine what a student has or has not learned. If a student were to miss the example item we would not be able to determine whether the student could correctly identify measures of central tendency, variability, or neither.

Express the statement as simply and clearly as possible.

Building on Thorndike's law of effect, Skinner believed that food, water, and smiling are examples of positive reinforcers.

Better:

Skinner believed that food, water, and smiling are examples of positive reinforcers.

As stated earlier about multiple-choice items, testing is a time to assess student learning, not to deliver content. Knowledge of the stated relationship between Skinner and Thorndike does little to enhance the student's ability to answer the item correctly. If this relationship is important you can test it in a separate item.

True-false items containing modifiers such as *usually, seldom,* and *often* are frequently true, whereas statements containing words such as *never, always,* and *every* are most likely to be false.

Repetition always strengthens the tendency for a response to occur. (false)

The process of extinction is seldom immediate but extends over a number of trials. (true)

Sense organs usually deteriorate in old age. (true)

Better:

Every word contains one or more morphemes. (true)

In a normal distribution the mean, median, and mode are always the same. (true)

Paranoia is usually treated by systematic desensitization. (false)

People are generally reluctant to believe that something is always or never true. Consequently, students are likely to respond false to statements with words such as *always* and *never*, and true to statements with words such as *usually* and *often*. To reduce the probability of students guessing correctly by following human instincts, several true-false items should be written for which true statements use *always* or *never* and false statements use *seldom* or *often*. Our purpose is not to trick students into missing an item but to better assess what they have learned.

Avoid using negatively worded statements.

Primary process thinking does NOT involve acting on the first thing that comes to mind.

Better:

Primary process thinking involves acting on the first thing that comes to mind.

True-false statements containing negative wording should be avoided because of the potential confusion with double negatives. In the example item, primary process thinking does involve acting on the first thing that comes to mind. The statement is better written in a positive direction (true/does) so as to avoid the double negative (false/doesn't).

False items tend to discriminate more highly than true items. Therefore, use more false than true items.

We all have a tendency to be yea-sayers or to agree with someone or something when searching for the correct response. Consequently, students are more likely to respond with a true when guessing on true-false items. To compensate for this human tendency, we recommend having more false responses be correct than true responses.

Activity: The next time you write true-false items use the following checklist to see which suggestions you followed.

_____ I based the true-false items on statements that are absolutely true or false, without qualifications or exceptions.

_____ I expressed the item statement as simply and as clearly as possible.

_____ I expressed a single idea in each test item.

_____ I included enough background information and qualifications so that the ability to respond correctly did not depend on some special, uncommon knowledge.

_____ I avoided lifting statements from the text, lecture, or other material.

_____ I avoided using negatively stated item statements.

_____ I avoided the use of unfamiliar language.

_____ I avoided the use of specific determiners such as *all, always, none,* and *never* and qualifying determiners such as *usually, sometimes,* and *often.*

_____ I used more false items that true items (but no more than 15% additional false items).

_____ I avoided language that may offend or exclude a particular group of individuals.

Matching Test Items

In general, matching items consist of a column of stimuli presented on the left side of the exam page and a column of responses placed on the right side of the page. Students are required to match the response associated with a given stimulus. Here's an example:

Directions: On the line to the left of each definition in Column I, write the letter of the defense mechanism in Column II that is described. Use each defense mechanism only once.

Column I (Stimuli)

1. _____ Hunting for reasons to support one's beliefs
2. _____ Accepting the values and norms of other's as one's own
3. _____ Attributing to others one's own unacceptable impulses or thoughts
4. _____ Ignoring disagreeable situations, topics, or sights

Column II (Responses)

A. Denial of reality
B. Identification
C. Introjection
D. Projection
E. Rationalization
F. Representation

Advantages of Using Matching Items

Matching items . . .

→ require short periods of reading and response time, allowing you to cover more content.
→ provide objective measurement of student achievement or ability.
→ provide highly reliable test scores.
→ provide scoring efficiency and accuracy.

Limitations of Using Matching Items

Matching items . . .

→ have difficulty measuring learning objectives requiring more than simple recall of information.
→ are difficult to construct due to the problem of selecting a common set of stimuli and responses.

Suggestions for Using Matching Items

Include directions that clearly state the basis for matching the stimuli with the responses. Explain whether or not a response can be used more than once and indicate where to write the answer.

Directions: Match the following.

Better:

Directions: On the line to the left of the theory of personality in Column I write the letter of the psychologist in Column II associated with the theory. Each psychologist in Column II can be used only once.

Students need to know exactly how to respond to the item, including whether or not responses can be used more than once.

Use homogeneous material in matching items, and if responses are not to be used more than once, include more responses than stimuli.

Directions: Match the following.

1. ＿＿＿ Food	A. Primary reinforcer
2. ＿＿＿ Psychoanalysis	B. Sigmund Freud
3. ＿＿＿ B. F. Skinner	C. Operant conditioning
4. ＿＿＿ Standard deviation	D. Measure of variability
5. ＿＿＿ Schizophrenia	E. Hallucinations

Better:

Directions: On the line to the left of the theory of personality in Column I write the letter of the psychologist in Column II associated with the theory. Each psychologist in Column II can be used only once.

1. ___ Psychodynamic Theory	A. Sigmund Freud
2. ___ Trait Theory	B. B. F. Skinner
3. ___ Behaviorism	C. Albert Bandura
4. ___ Humanism	D. Gordon Allport
5. ___ Social Learning Theory	E. Raymond Cattell
	F. Carl Rogers
	G. Karen Horney

The matching item provides an efficient way to test content. However, if the content is not homogeneous in structure the test becomes a contest of matching words or stimulus terms with response terms, without reference to content. In the example item, *mean* is matched with a statistical term, *schizophrenia* is matched with symptoms, a *psychologist* is matched with a theory, and so on. Also, if there are an equal number of responses and stimuli, and responses are not to be reused, students can make the last match through the process of elimination.

Arrange the list of responses in some systematic order if possible (e.g., chronological and alphabetical).

Directions: For the following set of numbers match the statistic in Column I with the correct calculation in Column II. Calculations in Column II can be used only once.

6 7 2 4 5 9 3 4 9 1 4

1. Mean	A. 9.0
2. Range	B. 4.9
3. Standard deviation	C. 4.0
4. Mode	D. 4.5
5. Median	E. 4.3
	F. 8.0
	G. 2.5

Better:

1. Mean   A. 9.0
2. Range   B. 8.0
3. Standard deviation   C. 4.9
4. Mode   D. 4.5
5. Median   E. 4.3
                           F. 4.0
                           G. 2.5

Students who know the correct answers can more efficiently select from the list of responses when they are presented in some systematic order. Students have told us that they are less likely to miscode an incorrect response on a separate answer sheet when the alternatives are ordered.

Keep matching items brief, limiting the list of stimuli to under 10, and when possible, reduce the amount of reading time by including only short phrases or single words as responses and stimuli.

Activity: The next time you write matching items use the following checklist to see which suggestions you followed.

_____ I included directions that clearly stated the basis for matching the stimuli with the response.

_____ I explained whether or not a response could be used more than once and indicated where to write the answer.

_____ I used only homogeneous material.

_____ When possible, I arranged the list of responses in some systematic order (e.g., chronologically and alphabetically).

_____ I avoided grammatical or other clues to the correct response.

_____ I kept items brief and limited the list of stimuli to under 10.

_____ I included more responses than stimuli.

_____ When possible, I reduced the amount of reading time by including only short phrases or single words in the response list.

_____ I avoided language that may offend or exclude a particular group of individuals.

Additional Objective Test Item Types

So far we have discussed common item types used by most classroom teachers. You should not limit yourself to these traditional item formats. Following are examples of other item formats that have not received very much attention but are clever and efficient measures of student achievement. Although we may think of these formats as new ways to test student learning, Carlson (1985) points out how many of these alternate formats were used in, 1930s and 1940s, before the emphasis on large-scale standardized testing became the norm.

Double Matching Items

Double matching items present two lists of response options to allow you to test two areas of knowledge. Here is an example of a double matching item.

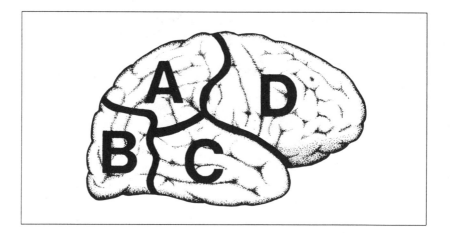

Sensory or Motor Function
   a. Vision
   b. Hearing
   c. Touch
   d. Motor behavior

Indicate the location and sensory or motor function of each of the following by writing the appropriate letter on each line.

Location in diagram (A-D)		Sensory or Motor Function (a-d)
_____	1. parietal lobe	_____
_____	2. temporal lobe	_____
_____	3. occipital lobe	_____
_____	4. frontal lobe	_____

Rank Order Items

The rank order item provides an efficient way to test student knowledge of the sequence or order of things such as stages of development. The following is an example of a rank order item.

Maslow believed that people would not be motivated to satisfy their higher needs until they had satisfied their lower needs. Order the following list of Maslow's needs from lowest (no. 1) to highest (no. 7).

_____ aesthetic needs

_____ cognitive needs

_____ safety needs

_____ physiological needs

_____ belongingness and love needs

_____ esteem needs

_____ self-actualization needs

Key List Item

The key list item is an extension of the simple checklist. Students can use a limited list of alternatives (the key list) to make repeated judgments about a series of statements. An example of a key list item is presented below.

For each of the following human defenses explained by psychodynamic theory, use letters to indicate whether the defense is a primary defense (P) or a secondary defense (S).

P = Primary defense
S = Secondary defense

_____ 1. repression
_____ 2. reaction formation
_____ 3. projection
_____ 4. denial
_____ 5. rationalization

Matrix Item

Matrix items are similar to simple matching items that have more than one response linked to a stimuli. A matrix item presents a table to students that lists responses vertically and stimuli horizontally. Students are instructed to check each cell in which the response across the top is true of each of the stimuli along the side. Here's an example of a matrix item.

Place an *X* in the appropriate squares to indicate the forms of thinking that are characteristic of Piaget's stages of mental development.

	Sensorimotor	Preoperational	Concrete Operations	Formal Operations
1. Focus on states				
2. Memory				
3. Conservation				
4. Accommodation				
5. Decentering				
6. Egocentrism				

Greater-Less-Same Items

Greater-less-same items provide an efficient way to test the relationship between two concepts. Different relationships can be tested, including relationships of time (which concept comes before or after the other) or size (which concept is greater than the other). An example of a greater-less-same item is provided below.

The following paired statements refer to behavior in Kohlberg's stages of moral development. If the moral behavior described on the left appears before the behavior on the right, circle the letter *B*; if the behavior on the left appears before the behavior on the right, circle the letter *A*; if the two behaviors, right and left, occur at about the same time according to Kohlberg, circle the letter *S*.

Obedience to rules to avoid punishment	B A S	Obedience to rules to obtain rewards
Obedience to democratically accepted laws	B A S	Morality of individual conscience
Seeking approval of others	B A S	Obedience to rules to obtain rewards

Interpretive Exercise Items

There are many variations of interpretive exercises. The following example illustrates a variation that requires students to interpret the contents in an illustration or written passage. These types of items are excellent measures of student achievement at the comprehension level of Bloom's Taxonomy.

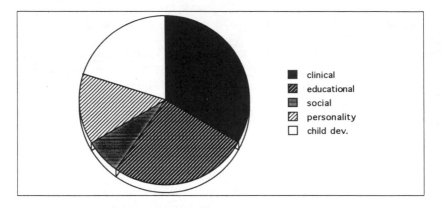

Percentage of Psychology Graduate Students by Contact Area:
1980-1990

The following statements refer to the data in the preceding graph. Read each statement and indicate your answer according to the following key.

Circle *S* if the statement is supported by the graph.
Circle *R* if the statement is refuted by the graph.
Circle *N* if the statement is neither supported nor refuted by the graph.

1. Approximately twice as many graduate students are studying educational than personality psychology.   S   R   N

2. Approximately one-third of the graduate students are studying clinical psychology.   S   R   N

3. Clinical psychology appears to be increasing in student popularity.   S   R   N

4 | Suggestions for Writing Constructed Response Test Items

The following types of constructed response test items are discussed in this chapter:

- Completion
- Essay
- Problem Solving

Completion Test Items

The completion item requires the student to answer a question or to finish an incomplete statement by filling in a blank with the correct word or phrase. Here are two examples of completion items.

What is the most common emotional reaction to stress?

_____

According to Freud, the mature view of sex is determined by how well the person handles the _____ stage.

Advantages of Using Completion Items

Completion items . . .

→ can provide a wide sampling of content.
→ can efficiently measure lower levels of cognitive ability.
→ can minimize guessing compared with multiple-choice and true-false items.
→ can usually provide an objective measure of student achievement or ability.

Limitations of Using Completion Items

Completion items . . .

→ are difficult to construct so that the desired response is clearly indicated.
→ have difficulty measuring learning objectives requiring more than simple recall of information.
→ can often include more irrelevant clues than other item types.
→ are more time-consuming to score than multiple-choice and true-false items.
→ are more difficult to score because more than one answer may have to be considered correct.

Suggestions for Using Completion Items

Clearly word the incomplete statement or question to elicit a unique response.

The ego strives to achieve satisfaction for the _____ in ways that are both moral and realistic.

Better:

The ego strives to achieve satisfaction for the id in ways that are both _____ and _____ .

Many different and correct responses could be placed in the first blank of the example item, such as person, id, or individual. Items should be written as clearly as possible to elicit only the response desired by the instructor.

Caution: You should be prepared to accept a variety of correct responses if you have written an ambiguous item.

Omit only significant words from the statement, but do not omit so many words from the statement that the intended meaning is lost.

Pharmacology is the science of _____ .

Better:

The science of drugs is called _____ .

Or:

The id is to _____ as the ego is to _____ .

Better:

The id is to pleasure as the ego is to _____ .

The purpose of the first example item is to test the definition of pharmacology; therefore, it may be a better strategy to ask students to recall the key term, which is *pharmacology*. What is the key relationship desired by the instructor in the second example item? As written, the second example poses an interesting challenge to see how many relationships about the id and ego students can identify. However, if you wanted to test the relationship between the id and its drive for pleasure and the ego's drive for reality, then the improved item would elicit the response desired.

Avoid grammatical or other clues to the correct response.

If Maria does not wash completely and change her clothes after a date, she becomes very anxious. Maria is suffering an _____ disorder.

Better:

If Maria does not wash completely and change her clothes after a date, she becomes very anxious. Maria is suffering a(n) _____ disorder.

The use of *an* in the example item may provide a grammatical clue to the correct answer of "obsessive-compulsive." Grammatical and other clues give an advantage to test-wise students.

When possible, delete words at the end of a statement rather than at the beginning.

_____ is the measure of central tendency that is least affected by extremely high or low scores.

Better:

Which measure of central tendency is least affected by extremely high or low scores? _____

The use of the complete question in the improved example item informs the student of the intent of the item and prepares the student to respond as he or she reads the question. The use of a blank at the beginning of an item often causes the student to read and reread the item to understand its intent. Unnecessary time and effort is spent when blank spaces are placed at the beginning of an item.

When using more than one blank space, make the fill-in lines the same length.

According to Freud, personality is made up of three mental structures, the _____, the _____, and the _____.

Better:

According to Freud, personality is made up of three mental structures, the _____, the _____, and the _____.

Spaces of unequal length provide a clue to the length of the desired responses. In the example, the clever student realizes that the question calls for two little words and a big word (the id, the ego, and the superego).

Use familiar language.

The phrase "the lady doth protest too much, methinks" most accurately refers to the defense mechanism called _____.

Better:

Briefly describe an example of a defense mechanism.

What first appears to be a clever test question becomes a source of confusion for one or more students. Words such as *doth* and *methinks* are not common knowledge to all students.

Activity: The next time you write completion items use the following checklist to see which suggestions you followed.

_____ I omitted only significant words from the statement.

_____ I did not omit so many words from the statement that the intended meaning was lost.

_____ I avoided grammatical or other clues to the correct response.

_____ I included only one correct response per item.

_____ I made the fill-in lines of equal length.

_____ When possible, I deleted the words at the end of the statement after the student was presented with a clearly defined problem.

_____ I avoided lifting statements directly from the text, lecture, or other source.

_____ I limited the required response to a single word or phrase.

_____ I avoided language that may offend or exclude a particular group of individuals.

Essay Test Items

A classroom essay exam consists of a small number of questions to which students are expected to demonstrate their ability to organize and present a logical, integrated answer to a question. An essay test item can be classified as either an extended-response essay item or a short-answer essay item. The latter calls for a more restricted or limited answer in terms of form or scope. An example of an extended-response essay item follows.

Explain the difference between the stimulus-response (S-R) and the stimulus-organism-response (S-O-R) theories of personality. Include in your answer (a) brief descriptions of both theories, (b) supporters of both theories, and (c) research methods used to study each of the two theories. (10 points)

Here is an example of a short-answer essay item.

Identify research methods used to study the stimulus-response (S-R) and stimulus-organism-response (S-O-R) theories of personality. (5 points)

Advantages of Using Essay Items

Essay items . . .

→ are easier and less time-consuming to construct than are most other item types.

→ provide a means for testing a student's ability to compose an answer and present it in a logical manner.

→ can efficiently measure higher-order cognitive objectives (e.g., analysis, synthesis, and evaluation).

Limitations in Using Essay Items

Essay items . . .

→ cannot measure a large amount of content or objectives.

→ generally provide lower test and test scorer reliability than do objective tests.

→ require an extensive amount of the instructor's time to read and grade.

→ generally do not provide an objective measure of student achievement or ability (subject to bias on the part of the grader).

Suggestions for Using Essay Questions

Prepare essay items that elicit the type of response desired.

Learning Objective. The student should be able to explain how the normal curve serves as a statistical model.

Describe a normal curve.

Better:

Briefly explain how the normal curve serves as a statistical model for estimation and hypothesis testing.

The essay question should be written to measure the content and level of learning targeted by the instructor. In the example item, the ambiguity of the question elicits a range of responses, some of which may be correct, but unrelated to the learning objective tested by the item. You should consider your learning objectives when developing corresponding test items.

Clearly explain the task required of the student.

Describe the difference between the stimulus-response (S-R) and the stimulus-organism-response (S-O-R) theories of learning.

Better:

Explain the difference between the stimulus-response (S-R) and the stimulus-organism-response (S-O-R) theories of personality. Include in your answer (a) brief descriptions of both theories, (b) supporters of both theories, and (c) research methods used to study each of the two theories. (10 points)

Students need to know what you are looking for in a response to an essay question. The example item was improved by indicating several elements to be included in a response. This additional information helps direct students' responses and prevent them from overlooking a critical element of the answer.

Indicate for each question the number of points earned for a correct response.

What are some major criticisms of the behavioral theory of alcoholism?

Better:

What are some major criticisms of the behavioral theory of alcoholism? (10 points)

Not all students finish an exam in the time provided. When time is running short it may be necessary for a student to leave 1 or 2 items unanswered. If forced to choose among items to leave blank, students may want to work on essays worth more points, provided this information is made available.

Avoid giving the student too much choice among optional items.

Directions: Respond to two of the following six questions.

Better:

Directions: Respond to five of the following six questions.

First, the use of only two essay questions severely limits the amount of content covered on an essay exam. Second, giving students a choice of responding to two of six essay questions also makes it impossible to discriminate between the student who could respond correctly to all six questions and the student who could answer only two. Third, having students respond to only two of six questions may also have a detrimental effect on scoring reliability. If you assign essay scores by comparing student responses (see Chapter 6), you may have difficulty making multiple comparisons if only one or two students respond to a particular item.

Despite content restrictions and reliability concerns, you may want to allow students a choice between questions so as not to penalize students who missed a particular lecture or do not understand one of the questions. We support this humanitarian approach but recommend asking students to choose four out of five or five out of six questions. In this way, content is less restricted and more students are likely to respond to each question.

Ask questions that will elicit responses for which experts could agree that one answer is better than another.

Students are sometimes able to bluff a correct essay response by providing a well-written answer to a related but different item (one that they know something about). This shouldn't occur if we know what a correct response should include. We ask particular questions to assess whether students know certain information; anything less than the desired information is incorrect or at best partially correct.

It is generally recommended that classroom exams administer several short-essay questions rather than one or two extended-response items.

The reason for this recommendation is the extended amount of coverage allowed by having several short-response essays rather than a few extended-response essays.

Activity: The next time you write essay items you can use the following checklist to see which suggestions you followed.

———— I prepared items that elicited the type of behavior I wanted to measure.

———— I phrased each item so that the student's task was clearly indicated.

———— I indicated for each item a point value.

———— I asked questions that elicited responses for which experts could agree that one answer is better than another.

———— I avoided giving the student too many choices among optional items.

———— I administered several short-answer items rather than one or two extended-response items.

———— I avoided language that may offend or exclude a particular group of individuals.

Problem-Solving Test Items

Another form of a constructed response test item is the problem-solving or computational exam question. Such items present the student with a problem situation or task and require a demonstration of work procedures and a correct solution. This kind of test item is classified as a constructed response type item because of the procedures used to score item responses. You can assign full or partial credit to either correct or incorrect solutions, depending on the quality and kind of work procedures presented. An example of a problem-solving test item follows.

The following test scores were collected from a sample of 14 athletes and 28 nonathletes:

Athletes	Nonathletes
$n = 14$	$n = 20$
Mean = 119	Mean = 116
$SD = 31.1$	$SD = 32.4$

Test the null hypothesis at the .01 level that the populations of athletes and nonathletes have equal test score means. Show your work for full or partial credit. (10 points)

Advantages of Using Problem-Solving Items

Problem-solving items . . .

→ minimize guessing by requiring the students to provide an original response rather than to select from several alternatives.

→ are easier to construct than are multiple-choice or matching items.

→ can most appropriately measure learning objectives that focus on the ability to apply skills or knowledge in the solution of problems.

→ can measure an extensive amount of content or objectives.

Limitations of Using Problem-Solving Items

Problem-solving items . . .

➡ require an extensive amount of instructor time to read and grade.
➡ may not provide an objective measure of student achievement or ability (subject to reliability on the part of the grader when partial credit is given).

Suggestions for Using Problem-Solving Items

Clearly identify and explain the problem, and provide directions that clearly inform the student of the type of response desired by the instructor.

Perform an analysis of variance for the following data based on four independent groups.

Better:

Perform an analysis of variance for the following data based on four independent groups. Provide an ANOVA summary table and state your conclusions about the result.

Just as with essay questions, you should write directions to problem items that clearly identify the type of response desired. You can inform the students of your intent to award points for an ANOVA summary table in the answer. We do not want to penalize capable students for omitting parts of an answer that were not directly requested in the question.

Clearly separate item parts and indicate their point totals, and state in the directions whether or not students should show their work for partial credit.

The following anxiety test scores were recorded for random samples of eight males and seven females. Test the null hypothesis at the .05 level of significance that males obtain higher anxiety scores than do females.

Better:

The following anxiety test scores were recorded for random samples of eight males and seven females. Test the null hypothesis at the .05 level of significance that males obtain higher anxiety scores than do females.

State the null hypothesis in numerical form. (2 points)
Calculate the obtained value of t. (1 point)
State the critical value(s) of t. (1 point)
State whether or not you reject the null hypothesis. (1 point)
In a sentence or two explain your results. (1 point)
Show your work to receive full or partial credit.

Some instructors do not believe in awarding partial credit or assigning points to parts of an answer. We have heard the engineering professor defend this position by saying a partially correct roof still falls down. However, we believe that students should have an opportunity to demonstrate what they know and receive credit for their knowledge. If you are concerned about the correctness of the final answer you can assign it the highest weight. Besides, you are in a better position to diagnose student errors by analyzing the parts of a response or studying the process used to develop the final answer.

Minimize errors caused by irrelevant calculation error by using whole or simple numbers in the problem and the answer.

A sample of 12 measurements of reaction time gave a mean of 7.38 seconds and a standard deviation of 1.24 seconds. Find the 99% confidence limits for the actual reaction time of the population tested.

Better:

A sample of 12 measurements of reaction time gave a mean of 9.0 seconds and a standard deviation of 2.0 seconds. Find the 99% confidence limits for the actual reaction time of the population tested.

The example item is intended to measure the student's ability to construct confidence intervals. The mathematics involved in the problem are secondary to the statistical procedure being tested. You can help students who are prone to making nervous errors on a timed test by using whole or simple numbers in the calculation of the problem. Complicated calculations may prevent you from determining whether students can or cannot construct a confidence interval.

Use figures, conditions, and situations that create a realistic problem.

Senior males from Southside High School averaged 29.0 on their ACT Assessment scores with a standard deviation of 30, whereas senior females averaged 33.0 with a standard deviation of 5.0. Use a t-test statistic to determine if the females significantly (p .05) outperformed the males.

Better:

Senior males from Southside High School averaged 29.0 on their ACT Assessment scores with a standard deviation of 4.0, whereas senior females averaged 33.0 with a standard deviation of 5.0. Use a t-test statistic to determine if the females significantly (p .05) outperformed the males.

Students are more capable of checking their work using a commonsense approach if the numbers used in a problem are realistic. In other words, calculation errors may be more obvious to the student in the example problem if he or she knows that a standard deviation cannot really be higher than the group mean.

Indicate the level of precision (e.g., numemical unit) desired in the answer, and work through each problem before classroom administration to double-check accuracy.

Activity: The next time you write problem-solving items use the following checklist to see which suggestions you followed.

_____ I clearly identified and explained the problem to the student.

_____ I provided directions that clearly informed the student of the type of response called for.

_____ I stated in the directions whether or not the student must show work procedures for full or partial credit.

_____ I clearly separated item parts and indicated their point values.

_____ I used figures, conditions, and situations that created a realistic problem.

_____ I asked questions that elicited responses for which experts could agree that one solution and one or more work procedures are better than others.

_____ I worked through each problem before classroom administration.

_____ I avoided language that may offend or exclude a particular group of individuals.

What is the next testing or grading activity? You have either developed new test items or selected items from existing sources. The next activity is to prepare your test and plan for its administration and scoring. Chapter 5 suggests ways to accomplish these activities.

5 | Preparing, Administering, and Scoring Classroom Exams

Discussion so far has focused on testing activities that included writing objectives, designing a test, and writing exam items. Activities involved in preparing, giving, and scoring the test are of equal importance. Although these activities are often considered routine, attention to the details of these activities can help you reduce the impact of two major problems instructors encounter in classroom testing: irrelevant sources of difficulty in the test and violations of academic integrity (cheating). In this chapter we take up the particulars on how to minimize these two problems.

Proper test preparation and scoring provides some degree of certainty that the test will function as the instructor intended. Failure to prepare and score exams properly can introduce measurement error (the part of test takers' scores that can be attributed to chance or irrelevant factors rather than knowledge of the content) and may decrease the validity of the inferences made about student achievement.

Carelessly planned or unplanned test administration can lead to violations of academic integrity. Several years ago, our office published a newsletter on how to prevent cheating. More than 3,000 faculty members requested the publication.

Obviously, how to deal with violations of academic integrity is a major concern to instructors. We will stress prevention strategies in this chapter, such as constructing two forms of the test or using seating arrangements. Why prevention? Ask any instructor who has dealt with cases of cheating, and they will tell you it is much easier to plan ways to prevent cheating than to deal with it later.

Making Classroom Exams

Using Existing Items

You often have access to existing items. Sources include department item files, item banks, instructor manuals, or items collected as a teaching assistant for courses. Previously written items can be a tremendous resource for an instructor. We strongly endorse using existing items with several cautions.

Follow the same procedures for selecting existing items that we suggested for developing new items. In other words, the items should specifically relate to your course content, objectives, and test specifications. Do not assume that items at the end of a textbook chapter or provided in the textbook item file will fit your test specifications. It is more likely the items will need some type of revision before they are suitable for your test. If you do find items that appear to fit your specifications, use the guidelines presented in Chapters 3 and 4 to inspect them for errors.

Activity: You might want to look at one of your exams for which you used items from other sources. Can you link your items with the course content and objectives? Evaluate the exam by using the item review checklists and the test review guidelines.

Item Arrangement

After the item review, you might think about how you want to sequence your test items on the exam. The following recommendations for arranging items on a test take into consideration item type, item difficulty, and item content. First, to warm up the students for test taking, we recommend selecting the two easiest items for the first two items on an exam. After selecting the first two items we recommend grouping the remaining items by item type to minimize careless errors by test takers and the number of test directions needed. In other words, all the fill-in-the-blank items are in one section, all multiple-choice items are in another section, and the essay items are placed in a third section of the test. This arrangement is essential when using machine-scorable answer sheets because it is not reasonable to expect students to complete multiple-choice items 1 through 14 on the answer sheet, complete fill-in-the-blank items 15 through 20 in the test booklet, and then return to the answer sheet for true-false items 21 through 25.

Once the exam is organized by item type, there are several strategies for arranging items within item type on the exam. Use the approach you find most appropriate. You can order items from easiest to most difficult or by increasing levels of taxonomic complexity. Most testing experts suggest that these arrangements optimize test performance by allowing all students to gain confidence as they go through the test. It is also beneficial from the instructor's point of view for diagnostic purposes. Grouping items according to difficulty makes it easier for you to identify student difficulties with particular learning outcomes.

Another strategy is to cluster items within item type by content area. This is also useful for diagnostic purposes because you can pinpoint specific areas of the course content that are problematic for students. Grouping by content also helps students organize their thoughts by working on one content area at a time. You could also combine the two strategies by grouping items by difficulty within item content.

Activity: Using one of your old exams try to determine your item arrangement. Did you have a scheme?

Test Directions

Test preparation also includes writing simple, concise test directions. Directions should include statements about:

→ how much time is available.
→ how to record answers.
→ whether to show work on problems.
→ point totals on different items.
→ whether there is a penalty for guessing.
→ whether texts, class notes, or calculators can be used during the test.
→ whether students can write comments or make notes in the test booklet.

Instructors often neglect to provide this type of information. Furnishing this information prevents misunderstandings about what you expect from your students, reduces irrelevant sources of difficulty, and minimizes questions during administration of the test. We also recommend that if you are using an answer sheet you provide directions on how to use these answer sheets on the test or a separate piece of paper. For example, our campus testing office provides written directions for instructors to use with machine-scorable answer sheets. The instructors duplicate these directions and distribute them for the first exam of the semester and for other exams, if necessary. Again, this is important in classes with students who may have minimal experience with machine-scorable answer sheets.

Decide in advance whether students are allowed to write in the test booklets or whether you are going to reuse them. Our preference is to allow students to mark in the booklet even if separate answer sheets are used. This allows students to note any items they find problematic and to communicate any concerns about the test. However, if the exam is lengthy, you may decide to use the test booklets again. You can then ask students to use notebook paper to record problems they have with specific items.

Because of limited resources for supplies, we have been told of instructors administering tests on overhead projectors. There are at least two major problems with this alternative. There is a limit on the amount of time the student has to respond to items and students do not have the opportunity to review specific test items at their own pace. Until there are other alternatives, such as computer-administered tests, we recommend individual administration of paper exams over group administrations using a projection device.

Test Assembly

We stress the importance of assembling a professional-looking examination. You want your students to take the exam process seriously and to try their best. The same could be said from the students' perspective. Administration of a poorly typed test with multiple mistakes and areas of confusion gives a message of carelessness and lack of effort on the part of the instructor. The following are some common test-assembly problems to avoid.

- Are there misspelled words and misnumbered items or pages?
- Are there typographical errors?
- Is there an item that has been split between two pages?
- Is the exam format consistent throughout the exam?
- Are there any format errors?
- Is there ample blank space for constructed response items?
- Are directions provided throughout the exam?

Such mistakes not only may be a source of distraction for students but can create problems in interpreting how an item and ultimately how the test functioned.

Activity: Pick up one of your old examinations to review or an exam you took as a student. Does it meet the criteria for a professional examination?

Constructing Alternate Forms

To encourage academic integrity and prevent cheating, we strongly suggest constructing alternate forms of each test. This is essential for large classes and highly recommended for smaller classes, especially with limited seating. (Other suggestions for preventing cheating are discussed later.) When constructing alternate forms you can do one of the following:

1. Vary the order of presentation for questions on the alternate forms.
2. Using the same items, scramble the order of the response alternatives for each item.
3. Present questions in a different order and scramble the order of response alternatives.

Generally, the first strategy listed above is sufficient for most testing situations. Presenting questions on alternate forms in different order is probably the simplest method. Strategies 2 and 3 require a significant amount of preparation time. There are a couple of precautions we want to mention with all three strategies. If you are using warm-up items (two easy items administered first), make the first two items identical on all forms and then reorder the remaining items. Also be aware that maintaining accurate keys can be difficult. Make sure to inform students in the directions to indicate their test form number on the separate answer sheet.

Administering the Classroom Exam

Planning for Test Taking (Administration)

Nothing is as disheartening to instructors as finding themselves in the position of having to deal with a violation of academic integrity. You can minimize these occurrences by constructing alternate forms and developing a set of procedures for administering the exam. In this section, we suggest some of these procedures. Although the strategies outlined below seem like extra work, they can be used to prevent problems before they occur.

From the instructor's point of view, the actual test administration is usually the simplest part of the testing process, if you have properly planned for the exam. To be fair to all students, before exam day, check the room where the exam is to be administered to ensure that the lights are functioning properly and make an assessment of the seating available to determine how to seat students for the exam. We list several other suggestions for administering exams below. These suggestions will not only help the test day go smoothly but reduce the opportunities for students to cheat.

1. If you are teaching a large class, make arrangements for your teaching assistants or, if available, proctors to assist you on exam day. The Instructional Development Office on our campus recommends a minimum of one proctor for every 40 students. Be sure the proctors keep moving around the room during the exam.

2. Seat students alternately (every other seat) if the space is available. If the desks can be moved, have students spread out throughout the room.

3. If desired, assign tests and seats by numbers.

4. Feel free to ask students to move and take seats in another part of the room.

5. Make sure you are distributing the alternate forms so different forms are distributed on all sides of students.

6. If you observe any activity among students that makes you uncomfortable, move the students immediately.

7. If the test is secure, plan on how you are going to have the tests returned so all the tests are returned to you.

8. Make sure students know how much time is allotted to complete the examination.

9. If the test is taking longer to complete than you expected, don't give extra time unless all students can remain.

10. If you do answer a question for a student during the exam, make this information available to all students. However, these should be kept to a minimum to avoid distractions for the other students.

11. Be careful not to direct students inadvertently to the correct answer when they ask about an item.

Avoid the Possibility of Cheating

Below are just a few commonly used cheating tactics that can be prevented by using proper test administration procedures.

1. Students share an eraser and test answers as they pass an eraser back and forth. *Prevention:* No sharing of pencils, erasers, calculators, and so on.

2. Students use the visors of their caps, shirt cuffs, and body parts to bring pertinent information into the exam. *Prevention:* Ask students to put caps under their desks and attempt to observe shirt cuffs, hands, and so on.

3. Students have a tape player and headphones that has pertinent information recorded. *Prevention:* No tape players.

4. Students arrange themselves at locations and angles to share test answers. *Prevention:* Assign seating arrangements to minimize this type of activity.

5. Student appears to take the exam but does not turn it in. The instructor assumes he or she lost the exam. *Prevention:* As the students turn in the exam, use the class roster to track who completed the exam.

Activity: How do you administer a classroom exam? Do you actively discourage violations of academic integrity with your test administration procedures? How?

Test Scoring

This section presents several considerations for scoring classroom examinations.

Activity: Take an old exam and review your scoring procedure. How did you assign points for your objective-type tests? Did you use a penalty for guessing? How did you score essay, short answer, and problem-solving test items? Can you explain to students how you score these types of items?

Differential Weighting of Items

Typically, objective items, such as true-false, multiple choice, and matching, are assigned one point for each correct answer. However, in an effort to represent the relative importance of specific content areas or items designed to measure knowledge at a specific level (e.g., application), instructors sometimes assign differential weights to items. Although differential weighting of items has a great deal of intuitive appeal, in practice, item weighting usually makes no difference in the rank order of students' scores. In other words, the student who scored the highest in the class will have the highest score whether some items are weighted more than others. Only the scale of the scores is changed. Differential item weighting adds a level of complexity to scoring that provides minimal benefits. Instead, if you consider one content area to be twice as important as another, write twice as many items to represent your content emphasis. If your course objectives stress application of knowledge, the number of application items you write should reflect this emphasis.

Correction for Guessing

Instructors frequently express concern about whether students are getting items correct on the basis of chance alone when they used objective-type items. To deter guessing, instructors adjust students' total scores by assessing a penalty for incorrect answers. This approach is commonly known as formula scoring. The penalty is usually a fraction of a point based on the number of incorrect answers (distracters) in the item. Here is the traditional correction-for-guessing formula:

$$\text{Total score} = \text{Number Right} - \frac{\text{Number Wrong}}{\text{Number of Distracters}}$$

This topic remains controversial with considerable disagreement among experts. Instructors assume students make guesses without any knowledge of the item content. It is our opinion that students are usually responding with at least partial information and are making educated rather than uninformed guesses. When distracters are carefully written, partial knowledge should lead to an incorrect answer because distracters should be attractive to partially informed students.

There can be a problem with guessing when most of the distracters are poorly written. Students can then select the correct answer by process of elimination. However, this is really not a guessing problem; it's a test-construction problem. Taking more care in writing distracters is the solution, not assessing a penalty for guessing. In general, assessing a penalty for guessing does not deter guessing and the relative ranking of students' scores remains the same whether a guessing penalty is used or not.

Scoring or Marking Constructed Response Items

A constructed response item is any item that calls for the test taker to construct the response rather than selecting the answer from several alternatives. Consequently, essay questions, short answer, performance measures, and problems requiring students to show their work all fall into this category.

There are basically two methods for scoring constructed response items: analytic and global quality scoring schemes. Either method is appropriate for each of the question types and need only to be adapted to the particular context. These approaches can also be used for any type of class project, such as research papers and performance assessments. Both schemes can be adapted to award partial or whole credit. You should select your scoring scheme before administering your test.

For an analytical scoring scheme, you construct an ideal answer in which specified elements are defined and assigned point values. You compare student responses to the ideal answer. Points are awarded when the student response contains the specified elements. The grade is based on the total number of accumulated points. You can require all elements to be present in the answer to receive credit (whole credit). Alternatively, if a student response contains only two of the five specified elements, you may award partial credit based on the elements present. Figure 5.1 is an illustration of both analytical and global scoring.

Using an analytical scoring approach, the sample item in Figure 5.1 is worth seven points. If the answer contains the concept of supply and demand, three points are awarded. If the relationship between supply and demand is specified an additional four points are awarded. Other answers are listed. These answers may also be partially correct and you need to decide whether any points will be awarded. Points may also be awarded for the clarity of the written response.

A global quality scoring scheme involves assigning a score (grade or points) based on either the total quality of the response relative to other student responses or the total quality of the response based on criteria you develop. A *stacks* method is illustrated in Figure 5.1 and is based on the notion of the total quality of response relative to other student responses. Here you briefly review all the papers and divide them into three stacks based on quality of response. The best papers are placed in stack 1, the average papers in stack 2, and the poorest papers in stack 3. You reread each stack and divide each original stack into two or three smaller collections of papers so there are finally six or nine stacks. Marks are then assigned to each of the stacks.

Quote:
"Americans are a mixed-up people with no sense of ethical values. Everyone knows that baseball is far less necessary than food and steel, yet they pay ball players a lot more than farmers and steel workers."

Question:
Why? Use three to four sentences to indicate how an economist would explain the above situation.

Scoring:

Analytical Scoring	Possible Points
Salaries are based on demand relative to supply of such services	3
Excellent ball players are rare	2
Ball clubs have a high demand for excellent players	2

Possible Credit:

Entertainment is as necessary as food or steel	1
Clarity of response	2

Global Quality Scoring:
Stacks

High   Medium   Low
/ | \   / | \   / | \
1 2 3   1 2 3   1 2 3

Figure 5.1. Scoring an Essay Item

The global quality scoring scheme based on the criteria developed by an instructor can be illustrated with an example from an introductory writing course. The criteria in the example distinguish between papers that will be assigned a 5 (the highest score) and a 4 (the next highest score).

Score	Criteria
5	Writing is consistently strong with sophisticated expression of ideas and/or advanced and original thought. There may be mechanical flows or inadequate logic or development but the power of expression overshadows these flaws.

4   Writing is strongly unified and well organized. There is adequate development of main ideas and effective use of illustration and argument. Areas that remain inadequate may include writing style (sentence structure and diction), original and sophisticated thought, use of sources, repetition, and redundancy.

One of our colleagues likes to tell a story about her first experience with global quality scoring. The first time she ever marked a set of papers she chose a scheme based on 1 to 5 points. A student who received a mark of 4 asked her why he did not receive a 5. She explained to him that it was a "4" paper. After much discussion, the instructor realized she could not explain why the paper was not given a mark of 5. Needless to say, it was an uncomfortable situation for both the instructor and the student.

You can avoid the type of problem our colleague described. If you developed a global scoring scheme similar to the writing example above, you can jot comments on students' papers based on the criteria. You not only will be giving students helpful feedback but will know why you assigned a 4 instead of a 5 if a student questions the mark. The same approach also is useful for the stacks method.

Pick the method that best fits your needs or philosophy. The analytical method is preferred over the global method for the inexperienced grader because the assignment of points is more explicit and objective. If you use a global quality scheme, be sure you can explain exactly how you scored the response so the process is understandable to students.

The most critical issue in scoring constructed responses is obtaining reliable or consistent results, not which method you use. A brainwashing example illustrates one aspect of this *intra*rater reliability problem. Suppose you scored all your constructed response items. Then you washed your brain and could not remember any scores you assigned. You then scored your items again. If the scores you assigned both times you marked the papers are identical or similar, the scores are reliable. Whether two different people (you and your teaching assistant) marking the same constructed response items will assign the same or similar scores is an example of *inter*rater reliability.

In the real world, you cannot clear your mind of past scoring efforts. However, we do have suggestions about how to address these concerns with reliability and list these along with other issues to think about when scoring constructed responses.

1. Be careful not to allow factors that are irrelevant to what is being measured affect your scoring. These factors, such as handwriting, neatness, and spelling should be considered only if they are identified as scoring elements or criteria. Research studies have shown these factors can affect how raters assign marks.

2. Read and score all student responses to one item before going on to the next item. In other words, score all the responses to Question 1 before reading Question 2. This helps to keep the frame of reference (the item) in mind when scoring all of the papers.

3. Score the tests without looking at the students' names to minimize the potential for personal bias (i.e., grading higher or lower than deserved).

4. Shuffle the papers while you are reading the answers to avoid order effects. (Sally's *B* work always followed Jim's *A* work so it always looks more like *C* work.)

5. When possible, ask a teaching assistant or colleague to read and grade a few of your students' responses to check scoring reliability. Verify your scores by rescoring several students responses. (If you can remember what you gave students' the first time, you have a good memory but not necessarily reliable scoring!)

6. Decide how to treat irrelevant or inaccurate information contained in students' responses. (Are you going to penalize inaccurate information and ignore irrelevant information?)

What is the next testing or grading activity? You have administered and scored your tests. The next activity is to evaluate the quality of the overall test and test items and, in the process, identify poorly written items that led to student confusion.

Chapter 6 suggests ways to evaluate your test and test items, address the problem of what to do with poor items, and communicate test results to your students.

6 | Evaluating the Quality of Classroom Exams

There are common questions that concern most instructors after they have administered and scored exams. These include the following: "Were there any problem areas or bad items?" "Was the exam any good, was it fair?" "Was it too easy or too hard?" Perhaps of greatest concern is "What am I going to say and do if the students think there is something wrong with some of the items or the whole exam?" A postadministration review of an exam can answer all of these questions and more.

A test review conducted after classroom administration can help you identify problematic items so you can make adjustments to total test scores and share the information with students when exams are returned. A test review can help you determine if the test was as difficult as planned and if it discriminated among students at different achievement levels. Examining how your test and the items performed can also give you feedback about yourself as a teacher and writer of test items. For instance, if you find most students are having problems with items at the application level or items pertaining to a certain content area, examine your instructional objectives and/or teaching strategies. You may determine that students did not have sufficient background to understand some item content and that they need to review or be retaught particular content areas.

Finally, test reviews prepare you for student concerns. After carefully reviewing student and test performance you know which items to defend and which to acknowledge as mistakes. Your careful review and analysis of each test item indicates to students that their test performance received a careful evaluation and that they were treated fairly.

The process we have described for developing course examinations involves a significant amount of work. The task becomes easier and the tests better if you take the time to review your tests before and after test administration. There will be some problems with your items that you missed during the test construction process. By evaluating the test and test items with the process we describe in this chapter, you will have clues as to which items are problematic and why the items are not functioning properly. You can then address major problems (e.g., incorrectly keyed items) immediately before assigning test scores and note minor problems (e.g., items with one or two unchosen distracters) for future reference.

The information collected from postadministration test reviews can be used to build an item bank of good and improved test items. Later in this chapter we demonstrate how instructors can build a bank of effective items. These banks can be established by keeping a record of how each test item performed. To minimize the amount of work in putting together exams, the banks or files can be referenced when writing exams. Over several testings you can build an item file that allows you to construct alternate forms of the test more efficiently.

Reviewing the Test With the Test Plan

Reviewing the test with the test plan involves looking at your test plan in relationship to numerical values that summarize how the test performed. These numerical summaries are usually referred to as test statistics. The test statistics are not meaningful unless you use the test plan as a context for interpreting them. Although all the test statistics can be calculated by hand, you will probably not have to do so. Many colleges and universities have their own examination systems or personal computer programs that provide you with item and test statistics at your request. If your college or university does not provide these services, several of these programs are available commercially at a moderate cost. They are worth investigating.

Exam Mean and Standard Deviation

There are several statistics calculated to examine the test overall. These include the mean, standard deviation, and the reliability coefficient. How you interpret these statistics depends on whether you constructed a norm-referenced or criterion-referenced test.

The mean is the familiar arithmetic average. You probably have an idea of how you expected students, on average, to perform on a test. If a test is too difficult or too easy, you will not be able to discriminate reliably between high-, middle-, and low-achieving students. The standard deviation refers to the spread of the test scores. It is the average amount by which test scores deviate from the mean of test scores. A large standard deviation indicates the scores are widely spread throughout the range of scores. A small standard deviation indicates that scores tend to cluster around the mean. You want a large standard deviation with a norm-referenced test because you want to make sure you have tested across all achievement levels so you can distinguish among these levels (e.g., the *A*, *B*, and *C* levels). With a criterion-referenced test, because you are comparing student performance to a standard, you may have a small standard deviation if most students are meeting the standard.

Exam Reliability

Reliability refers to the consistency of scores. When assessing student performance, you want some degree of assurance that if you gave the students another test covering the same material that the rank order of scores would be similar. Usually, for norm-referenced tests, a reliability estimate is a correlation coefficient that ranges from 0 to 1. A correlation coefficient is an index that indicates the degree of the relationship between two sets of scores. Generally, the test score reliability coefficient calculated for classroom tests is the Kuder-Richardson method, a measure of internal consistency. This test score reliability coefficient estimates the extent to which the items in the test are assessing the same content. If your test is homogeneous, that is, all the items are measuring highly related content areas, your reliability estimates are likely to be high. However, if the items are designed to measure more diverse content, the reliability coefficient will be lower. Although high reliability coefficients are desirable (.80 to .90+), they can be difficult to achieve with most classroom examinations when you are beginning to develop your item bank. Reliability estimates in the .70's are quite acceptable. If your test content is heterogeneous, even lower estimates are tolerable (.65+). However, as you refine your items and readminister them, you can expect and should see the test score reliability increasing.

Activity: Take an old exam and look at the mean, standard deviation, and the reliability coefficient. Is the mean about what you expected? Is the standard deviation small or large? Was your exam a norm-referenced or criterion-referenced test? What was your test score reliability? Was your test content heterogeneous?

Reviewing the Test Items
With the Test Plan

Item analysis is an examination of item performance. Judgment about an item consists of both a quantitative and qualitative review. The quantitative review involves examining item statistics that are numerical summaries of item performance. The qualitative review refers to reading the item's stem and responses in the context of their statistics. We do not recommend limiting your review to a quantitative analysis only. Any decision to eliminate or modify an item should be based on a review of its statistics and the text of the item.

Like the test statistics, all the item statistics can be hand calculated. Again check with your college or university to see what kinds of exam services are available.

Item Statistics

Item Difficulty

The item difficulty is the percentage or proportion (typically identified as a p-value) of students who answered an item correctly. Imagine you administered an item to 10 students. If 6 students answered the item correctly, the item difficulty is .6, or 60% of the students selected the correct response. Obviously, this value can be calculated for each item on a test.

What is a "good" item difficulty? There is no single value that is an indicator of whether an item difficulty is good or poor. Certainly, a item difficulty of .10 indicates the item was quite difficult whereas .90 indicates the item was particularly easy. If you construct a norm-referenced test, you want a range of item difficulties so you can distinguish among different levels of achievement reliably. If a considerable number of your items have an item difficulty of .90 (for a norm-reference test), your test is probably too easy. On the other hand, this may not be the case if you constructed a criterion-referenced test, reflecting student achievement of standards. If many of your test items reflected material that was relatively easy, most of your students may be mastering that material. In addition, the item statistics from difficult concepts will look like the items were easy if your students have

Table 6.1 Sample Size and Score Ranges by Quintile

Quintile	Sample Size	Score Range
1st	128	77 to 92
2nd	127	70 to 76
3rd	121	64 to 69
4th	121	56 to 63
5th	106	24 to 55

mastered those difficult concepts. This kind of distinction requires your professional judgment.

In general, a good item differentiates between students who score high and low on the test overall. You want to make sure that the higher-scoring students are answering the item correctly and that lower-scoring students are selecting the distracters or incorrect alternatives. As a first step in determining this, you can divide the class into groups based on total test score. To compare different student performance levels on the examination, classes can be divided into thirds, quartiles (quarters), or quintiles (fifths). While this is a great deal of work to do on your own, this type of table is readily available from most computerized item analysis packages. Table 6.1 is an example of a quintile table that is constructed by our campus's computerized item analysis program. The first fifth includes students who scored between the 81st and 100th percentiles (indicating 80% of the students scored lower on the test than this group). The second fifth includes students who scored between the 61st and 80th percentiles, and so forth. Table 6.1 also indicates the sample size, and the score ranges within each fifth for a sample test.

Once the class has been divided into groups, you can look at what proportion of students are answering the item correctly within each group or quintile with a graph. Again, we do not recommend that you graph each item. Rather most computerized item analyses packages produce a graph for each item automatically. Figure 6.1 presents a graph of the propor-

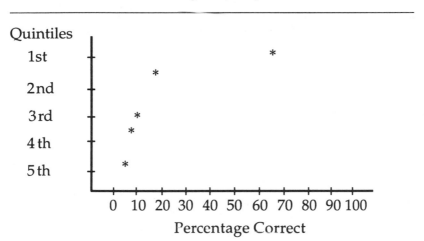

Figure 6.1. Percentage of Students Answering Correctly on Item 1

tion of students selecting the correct response for the following item (Item 1).

Item 1. Alex, in the movie *The Morning After*, is most like
  a. Kirsten.
  b. Angie.
  c. Lillian Roth.
  d. Frankie.

As you can see from Figure 6.1, more than 60% of the students in the first quintile (containing the highest scoring students) selected the correct response. In contrast, only 5% of the students in the bottom quintile (containing the lowest scoring students) answered the item correctly. This is a desirable feature in an item. You want to see more students answering the item correctly going from the fifth to first quintile. However, as you can see from the graph, there is only a 10% difference between students in the fifth quintile and second quintile. This is a difficult item that separates the highest-performing students from the rest of the students. If all of your

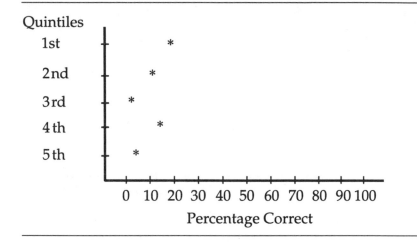

Quintiles

Percentage Correct

Figure 6.2. Percentage of Students Answering Correctly on Item 2

test items perform like this, you will not be able to distinguish reliably between the medium- and lower-achieving students.

Item 2. The "happy drunk" keeps alive the myth of
    a. wine and roses.
    b. normal social drinking.
    c. negative drunken comportment.
    d. alcohol being a nonequivocal spirit.

The graph for the answers to Item 2 in Figure 6.2 presents the proportion of correct responses for an item that clearly is problematic. As you can see by the graph, less than 25% of the students in the top quintile answered this item correctly. In addition, a higher percentage of students in the fourth quintile are selecting the correct response compared with the students in the second and third quintile. The graph enables us to identify a problem. Unfortunately, it does not necessarily help us understand why the problem exists.

Table 6.2 Matrix of Responses by Fifths for Item 2

Quintile	A	B	C	D	Omitted
1st	3	14	42	0	0
2nd	4	11	57	0	0
3rd	6	4	51	0	0
4th	2	9	39	0	0
5th	7	6	46	0	0
Proportion	0.07	0.15	0.77	0.00	0.00

NOTE: Alternative B is the correct response.

Distracter Analysis

To diagnose problems, the proportion of students selecting the distracters can also be calculated to assess how the distracters are functioning. This can be compared with the proportion of students selecting the correct response. You want to see what proportion of which groups are selecting the correct answer and distracters. Again, these calculations can be carried out by a computer program and arranged in a table of responses. A distracter analysis for the problematic Item 2 is presented in Table 6.2.

In Table 6.2, the response options A, B, C, D, and Omitted head the columns. For this item, B was the correct response. The numbers in the rows marked 1st, 2nd, 3rd, and so forth are the numbers of students in the quintile who selected the response. For example, 14 students in the first quintile selected B, the correct response. The largest number of students in each quintile selected C, an incorrect response. No test takers choose D, and no students omitted this item.

The value next to the row marked "proportion" is the proportion of students choosing the particular response alternative. The item difficulty of Item 2 (the proportion of students selecting alternative B) is 0.15, indicating this is a difficult test item for which only 15% of the students got the item correct. A total of 77% of the students were wrong in selecting alternative C.

How can this information help us to decide whether this item is functioning properly? This information shows which distracters are not successful, because few or no students chose the alternative (see alternative *D*). The table of responses also indicates that 77% of the students were attracted to the wrong answer in alternative *C*. From the numerical summary alone, you do not know whether this is a good distracter or whether there is something ambiguous. When you are reviewing your item analysis and find this kind of problem, it is critical at this stage to review these numerical summaries in relationship to the text of the item. Read the item again knowing that a large portion of the class selected one distracter. Was alternative *C* actually correct? Did you miskey the item? Review your test specifications and see if you meant this to be a difficult item, one written at least at the application level. You are the one who decides whether it is ambiguous or whether you wrote a great distracter.

Item Discrimination

For a good item, students in the upper fifths will answer with the correct response more frequently than students in the lower fifths, and students in the lower fifths will answer with an incorrect alternative more frequently than students in the upper fifths. A visual inspection may give you some sense of whether the item discriminated between low- and high-achieving students. There is, however, an item statistic called the discrimination index that places a numerical value on the item's ability to discriminate. Discrimination indices are indicated in Table 6.3 as RPBI values, also called point-biserial correlations.

The point-biserial correlation indicates the relationship between the item response and the total test score within the group tested. High positive RPBIs for the correct responses would represent the most discriminating items. That is, students who responded correctly to a particular item scored well on the entire exam, whereas students who responded incor-

Table 6.3 Matrix of Responses by Fifths for Item 2: Discrimination Analysis

Quintile	A	B	C	D	Omitted
1st	3	14	42	0	0
2nd	4	11	57	0	0
3rd	6	4	51	0	0
4th	2	9	39	0	0
5th	7	6	46	0	0
Proportion	0.07	0.15	0.77	0.00	0.00
RPBI	−0.06	0.08	−0.01	0.00	−.15

NOTE: Alternative *B* is the correct response.

rectly to the item did not score well on the entire exam. It is also interesting to check the RPBIs for the item distracters, or incorrect alternatives. The opposite correlation between total score and choice of alternative is expected for the incorrect responses. When a positive correlation is desired for the RPBI of a correct alternative, a negative correlation is good for the RPBI of a distracter, that is, students who answer with an incorrect alternative did not score well on the total examination.

As you can see in Table 6.3, Item 2 does not discriminate well among test takers. The point-biserial correlation between the correct answer and the total score is 0.08, indicating poor discrimination. The most often chosen distracter, *C*, also failed to discriminate among ability levels as indicated by its low RPBI. In this particular case, after reviewing test specifications and the actual item, the instructor decided to drop the item from the exam. This happens to all of us, especially if it is the first time the items are administered. Although this item was meant to be difficult and *B* was the correct answer, the instructor determined after reviewing the item content, the item was beyond the reach of even the high-scoring students.

How do you write discriminating items? To maximize item discrimination, items of moderate difficulty level are preferred, although easy and difficult items still can be discriminating. Table 6.4 contains a distracter analysis for Item 1, including the

Table 6.4 Matrix of Responses by Fifths for Item 1: Discrimination Analysis

Quintile	A	B	C	D	Omitted
1st	83	35	10	0	0
2nd	19	85	23	0	0
3rd	17	67	37	0	0
4th	13	78	30	0	0
5th	6	64	16	0	0
Proportion	0.23	0.57	0.19	0.00	0.00
RPBI	0.43	−0.33	−0.05	0.00	0.00

NOTE: Alternative A is the correct response.

RPBI for the correct response and distracters. Although Item 1 is also a difficult item, the correlation between the item responses and the total score for the correct answer is positive and substantial (0.43). As you can see from the RPBI, the B distracter is particularly effective. The correlation (−0.33) is again large but negative, indicating students with lower scores selected this distracter. The RPBI for response option C is reasonable, especially because B is functioning so well.

In contrast to Item 2, Item 1 performed as the instructor planned. As indicated in the test specifications and the review of the item content, the instructor expected this item to be one of the most difficult on the test and it discriminated quite well between highest-achieving students and the rest of the students.

Special Concerns About Item Analysis

When reviewing your item analysis, it is important to consider how many students took the test when interpreting the statistics. If you have a class of 500, you can be reasonably certain that the item statistics are accurate and not influenced by idiosyncrasies of a small sample. This is not the case when you have a smaller number of test takers. We recommend extreme caution when interpreting item statistics with classes smaller than 25 students. They should be considered primitive indicators of item performance. We advise prudence when you examine an item analysis from a class of 25 to 50 students. Be sure any decision you make about item performance is supported by both your qualitative and quantitative review.

Items With Low Point-Biserial Correlations

We discussed the importance of discriminating items in some detail. We want to issue a caution about the interpretation of the point biserial. Items with low point biserial should not automatically be deleted from your test or from your item bank. Instead, you need to inspect the actual item and the test specifications to interpret RPBIs. If you have an item with an item difficulty of 0.70 or greater and an RPBI less than 0.25 and the concept you are testing is basic, the item is probably fine. If the item is testing a simple concept from the reading that you did not cover in class, it is probably functioning properly. (You may have caught some of the higher-achieving students not doing the reading, and you are rewarding the lower-achieving students who did.) However, you do not want the majority of your items to have these types of statistics. As we mentioned earlier, you will have difficulty distinguishing between lower- and higher-performing students if most of your items fail to discriminate.

Handling Clinkers

Clinkers are problem items that for various reasons do not perform as you intended. Item 2 is an example of a clinker. It is almost impossible to construct a test with new and untried items without having several (five or less) items turn out to be clinkers. Instructors need to be aware this is likely to happen and be prepared to take action when it occurs. You make these decisions about clinkers based on an inspection of the test question and the item analysis.

With many poor items you can either accept more than one response as a correct answer or decide to drop the item from the test. If the problem with an item is that there are two correct answers, the test can simply be rescored so that both answers are counted as correct. Instructors inform students that there are two correct answers to the item when the exam is returned. However, this strategy is appropriate only if the two answers are genuinely correct. For a clinker item, some instructors drop the item altogether, whereas others drop the item and then add one point to each test taker's total score. However, this strategy is appropriate only if the item analysis indicates the test takers' responses to the item are aberrant. It is most unusual to have most of the low-achieving test takers answer an item correctly and the high-achieving test takers answer it incorrectly.

Occasionally, instructors use the item analysis to purify the test. This involves scoring and rescoring the exam several times, dropping items after each rescore. This approach is not justifiable and can be unfair to students at all achievement levels.

If you have several items that are problematic (and this can happen), you want to examine them very carefully in relation to your test specifications as a group. If the malfunctioning items are scattered randomly throughout the test specifications, then you should not be too concerned. However, if you find that several items related to one content area did not function properly, then you can't be sure how much of that content students have learned. Alternatively, if you find that items written at the higher levels of knowledge, such as the application level, were problematic, you cannot make the inference that students can apply the material that you covered in your course. To address this, you can quiz students or give other assignments to assess students' mastery.

Handing the Exam Back to the Students

When the test and item analyses are completed and changes are made (if needed), the exam results are ready to be returned to students. Like test administration, proper planning for this part of the testing process is worthwhile. Allowing ample time for students to ask questions about the exam, for clarifying any misconceptions, and providing feedback about their performance makes the test a learning experience as well as gives students the sense they are being treated fairly.

Pass out a copy of the exam to each student with a listing identifying which items he or she missed, what his or her response was, and the correct answers. The exam services at many universities prepare individual student score reports when exams are machine scored. Plan time to go over each exam question. Allow students to keep a copy of the exam only if you plan on never using any of the test questions again. The in-class test review can provide the opportunity for instructors to learn how well the students understand the course material and the types of misconceptions they have.

During the in-class review, be prepared to acknowledge some clinker items if there are some and areas that need additional review. Welcome student critiques, but know when to cut off discussion by inviting students to discuss their concerns after class. We still remember the new assistant professor who once asked us, "What do you do if the students become violent?" We assured him of his safety and reminded him students appreciate an instructor who is willing to discuss his or her test openly.

We encourage instructors to collect student feedback about their classroom exams. Although this can be conducted at the end of course evaluation, we find it helpful to ask student opinion during the course, particularly after the first exam. This information can be gathered during the exam review by asking students to write on the exam any areas of question and concern or to complete a short evaluation form. Here are some evaluation items about testing that may be included on a student evaluation form.

How would you rate the instructor's examination questions?

Excellent   Poor

    5   4   3   2   1

How well did examination questions reflect content and emphasis of the course?

Well related   Poorly related

    5   4   3   2   1

The exam reflected important points in the reading assignments.

Strongly agree   Strongly disagree

    5   4   3   2   1

Examination mainly tested trivia.

Strongly agree   Strongly disagree

    5   4   3   2   1

Were exam questions worded clearly?

Yes, very clear   No, very unclear

    5   4   3   2   1

Were the instructor's test questions thought provoking?

Definitely yes   Definitely no

    5   4   3   2   1

Did the exam challenge you to do original thinking?

Yes, very   No, not
challenging   challenging

    5   4   3   2   1

Were there trick or trite questions on the test?

Lots of them   Few if any

   5   4   3   2   1

How difficult was the examination?

Too difficult   Too easy

   5   4   3   2   1

I found I could score reasonably well on the exam just by cramming.

Strongly agree   Strongly disagree

   5   4   3   2   1

How was the length of exams for the time allotted?

Too long   Too short

   5   4   3   2   1

Was the exam (papers, reports) returned with errors explained or personal comments?

Almost always   Almost never

   5   4   3   2   1

Was the exam adequately discussed upon return?

Yes, adequately   No, not enough

   5   4   3   2   1

Item Banking or Item Filing

There are several different approaches available for establishing an item bank or item file, ranging from simple to complex. The simplest approaches involve keeping a written record that usually includes the following information:

ITEM 1

    Topic: The Female Alcoholic   Date Administered: July 1992

                                                    Level: Analysis

    Alex, in the movie *The Morning After,* is most like

        23%   0.48

    A. Kirsten

    B. Angie

    C. Frankie

    D. Lillian Roth (replace this distracter)

Correct response is *A.*

Figure 6.3. Example of an Item Bank Entry Entered on an Index Card

- Item stem
- Response options
- Content area of the item
- Test objective or level of item
- Item analysis information
- Administration dates

Typically the item bank information is recorded on an index card. Figure 6.3 is an example of this approach.

The correct answer *A.* The item statistics indicate this is a difficult, highly discriminating item, because only 23% of the students got this item correct and the point-biserial correlation is 0.48. If one of the distracters performed poorly, it should be indicated on the item record. We like to maintain a record of poorly performing distracters so we do not inadvertently use them again.

Using the simple approach described above is an adequate way to bank items. Instructors may want to investigate whether their college or university makes available computerized item banking. If not, there are several item banking computer packages that are commercially available. These packages generally provide item and test analysis, storage of items and item analysis results, and print capabilities. Depending on the software capabilities, you can use such programs to bank items by content and test objective so that items can be selected from the bank by content area and level of learning.

What is the next testing and grading activity? You have evaluated your test and handled problem items appropriately. You are ready to assign grades on the basis of the test scores and other grading components. In Chapter 7 we suggest ways to develop a grading strategy and describe and critique several grading methods.

7 | Assigning Grades

All instructors have a desire to assign grades that genuinely reflect students' achievement in a course. However, most instructors would much rather face three revisions of a manuscript than be asked how they assign course grades. How do you deal with students who question their course grades? If you feel defensive and unsure of yourself, you are not alone. Perhaps it is the "tweeners" that are disturbing. These are grades that are on the borderline, for example, A−/B+. Are you comfortable justifying your course grade assignments as long as the grade is a solid *A*, *B*, or *C*? Is it your policy always to assign the higher grade if the student is particularly attentive in class? Maybe you have a general feeling of uneasiness. For instance, do you find that sometimes you are surprised after you add up students' scores that some students are doing better than you thought while others are doing worse?

This chapter addresses these concerns. The purposes of grading and specific grading issues are discussed. Guidelines you can use to develop a grading strategy are presented. How to develop a grading strategy with which you are comfortable is specified on a step-by-step basis.

Purposes of Grading

According to several early studies, the first grading system was implemented at Yale in 1785 to describe their students. The procedure was composed of qualitative indicators of performance that included four categories: optimi, second optimi, inferiores (boni), and pejores. In general, the first campus grading systems were designed to let students know how the professors thought they performed on the exam. Today, although grading has multiple functions, a primary purpose of a course grade is still to communicate to students the level of achievement attained in the course. In turn, grades assigned to coursework or tests are designed to communicate to students how they are currently performing in the class.

Grades are also used to make important decisions. McKeachie (1986) suggests students use course grades to decide if they should take more courses in an area, to determine what their major should be, and if the area is an appropriate career choice. Administration uses grades to award honors and scholarships and grant admission to programs. Prospective employers use grades as a proxy for predicting job performance. Clearly grades have a significant impact on the career trajectory of students. Consequently, instructors have an obligation to assign grades fairly and accurately to students. When grading policies and practices are carefully formulated and reviewed periodically, grades provide legitimate information in the decision-making process. If instructors fail to state and adhere to explicit criteria for making grade assignments, then grades may convey incorrect information about student achievement and lead students and decision makers astray.

Grading Issues

Instructors often find grading to be one of the most difficult teaching responsibilities and a significant source of anxiety.

Perhaps the major reason for instructors' concerns is that grading requires instructors to make value judgments about how to assign grades. Establishing fair and accurate grading policies and procedures involves answering difficult questions.

- What do course grades represent?
- What proportion of the class should receive *A*'s, *B*'s, *C*'s, *D*'s, and *F*'s and how is the proportion determined?
- What strategy is followed when assigning grades?
- How should the achievement indicators (tests, homework, and papers) be weighted and combined to determine the final course grade?

In spite of the fact the assignment of course grades usually involves some kind of rank order summary of performance (e.g., *A, B, C, D, F* or 5, 4, 3, 2, 1), there are no empirical studies that support one method for ranking students over another. Instead, the development of a ranking or grading strategy requires considerable reflection by instructors. Here we offer some suggestions for developing a grading strategy.

Developing a Grading Strategy

An individual instructor's own attitudes, values, and assumptions influence his or her grading policies and practices. When we present workshops on grading we administer a quiz that reveals some of instructors' attitudes, values, and assumptions that influence their grading. We find the quiz often serves as a good starting point for instructors to evaluate how they grade.

Activity: Take the quiz that follows. The results will give you some notions of your values, attitudes, and assumptions about grading.

Grading Quiz: Do You Agree (A) or Disagree (D)?

1. Assigning grades is a handicap to learning.   A   D
2. The majority of instructors rely too much on   A   D
   their ability to judge grading and evaluating.
3. Instructors should attempt to grade and   A   D
   evaluate students in such areas as attitudes,
   attendance, and motivation.
4. Absolute grading (whereby students are   A   D
   compared to a standard rather than each
   other's performance) is as likely to stimulate
   student efforts to achieve as is relative grading.
5. Absolute grading strategies should allow   A   D
   each student the opportunity to receive an *A*.
6. An instructor's grading strategy should   A   D
   account for errors in measuring the various
   grading components.
7. Course grades should include diverse   A   D
   components, such as homework, projects,
   and test scores.

Our Answers

1. DISAGREE   While this belief receives considerable
                attention, we do not believe assigning grades
                is a handicap to learning. Grades, in fact,
                provide information, motivate, and aid
                students in finding out about their particular
                areas of strength and weakness. Grades do
                not distort learning or teaching when used
                properly.

2. AGREE   Assigning grades requires judgment, but
                grading criteria should be written such that
                other individuals would reach the same judg-
                ment as your own. In other words, the final
                judgment should not be a mystery to all but
                yourself. When grading criteria are defined

explicitly and communicated to the students, final grades are more objective and grades are more likely to represent what they are supposed to represent—student achievement.

3. DISAGREE   Instructors can assess students in such areas as attitude, attendance, and motivation and communicate the results of this assessment by letters of recommendation, oral interviews, and written feedback on class assignments. The purpose of grading is to communicate to students how well they mastered the course material, not whether they attended class or were motivated and not to provide information about their attitudes.

4. AGREE   Although instructors assume that relative grading (comparing a student's performance to the performance of other students in the class) is critical to motivating students to achieve, research suggests that absolute grading (comparing a student's performance to a set of standards) is also motivating to students. In fact, relative grading can be so competitive, it may be debilitating to achievement motivation. In contrast, students under absolute grading systems compete to meet standards at no cost to one another.

5. AGREE   Absolute grading strategies, by definition, offer each student the opportunity to receive an A, because performance is compared to a set of standards. However, it is highly unlikely that this will occur because of student differences in ability, previous coursework, motivation, interest in the topic, and experience out of the classroom.

6. AGREE   In spite of all your efforts, there is some error of measurement in all grading components.

This is not an issue unless student performance is on the borderline between two grades. To address this problem, a grading strategy can be designed to contain what is typically called a fudge factor. The fudge factor is a consistent indicator of student performance, such as homework assignments, for making the decisions in borderline cases. We do not recommend instructor's professional judgment, which is another approach that is also used for borderline cases.

7. AGREE   Measuring student performance in several contexts contributes to measurement accuracy. Mastery of some course objectives (e.g., performance type) simply cannot be assessed with in-class exams. In addition, some students are clearly more comfortable with some assessment methods than others. For instance, some students prefer essay items over multiple choice. Other students have difficulty doing their best work in the traditional classroom exam setting. Projects offer an additional way for students to demonstrate their understanding of the course material.

In addition to your own values, attitudes, and assumptions, other factors should be taken into account when grading. Factors such as instructional goals and course design (introductory or advanced) and institutional context such as department, college, or campus policies may impact the specific grading approaches instructors select.

Golden Rules of Grading

Although all grading strategies are highly individualized, grading strategies should be characterized by what we call the golden rules of grading.

- Fairness
- Accuracy
- Consistency
- Defensibility

By fair, we mean each student has an equal opportunity for each grade. When all tests, papers, and other assignments are thoughtfully prepared and scored, a grading strategy is likely to be accurate. A grading strategy that is planned and presented to students at the beginning of the semester and is not changed without considerable reflection is consistent. Finally, a grading strategy is defensible when interested parties can understand the instructor's explanation of why one student was assigned an *A* while another student received a *B*.

Activity: Look at the way you assigned course grades for one of your courses. Could your approach to assigning grades be characterized as fair, accurate, and consistent? Is your grading approach defensible?

Basic Grading Guidelines

Several years ago staff from our campus testing office (Office of Instructional Resources, 1979) asked faculty on campus to help identify a set of guidelines to follow when developing a grading strategy. Through the years we have presented these guidelines at numerous instructional workshops with little disagreement or changes requested by the participants. New and continuing instructors continue to find them useful.

Guideline 1: Grades should conform to the practice in the department and the institution in which the grade occurs.

Grading policies of the department, college, or campus may limit the grading procedures that can be used and require a basic grading approach for all instructors in that unit. Departments often have written statements that specify a method of assigning grades and meanings of grades. If such grading policies are not explicitly stated or written for faculty use, the percentages of A's, B's, C's, D's, and F's given by departments and colleges in their courses may be indicative of implicitly stated grading policies. Grade distribution information is usually available from departmental offices at all colleges and universities. Instructors find it is well worth their time to review this type of information. New or continuing faculty can consult with the department head for advice about grade assignment procedures in particular courses as another source of information about grading policy.

Guideline 2: Grading components should yield accurate information.

Carefully written tests and/or graded assignments (homework, papers, and projects) are keys to accurate grading. Because it is not customary at the university level to accumulate many grades per student, each grade carries great weight and should be as accurate as possible. Poorly planned tests and assignments increase the likelihood that grades will be based primarily on factors of chance. No evaluation efforts can be expected to be perfectly accurate, but there is merit in striving to assign course grades that most accurately reflect the level of competence of each student.

Guideline 3: Grading plans should be communicated to the class at the beginning of each semester.

By stating the grading procedures at the beginning of a course, you are essentially making a contract with the class about how each student is going to be graded. The contract should provide the students with a clear understanding of the instructor's expectations so that students can structure their work efforts. Students should be informed about which course activities will be considered in their final grade. Information about the importance or weight of exams, quizzes, homework sets, papers, and projects should also be provided. Advise students of the relative importance of the topics covered in the course. Students also need to know what method will be used to assign their course grade and what kind of comparison the course grade will represent. All of this information can be communicated effectively as a part of the course outline or syllabus.

Guideline 4: Grading plans stated at the beginning of the course should not be changed without thoughtful consideration and a complete explanation to the students.

Two common complaints found on students' postcourse evaluations are that grading procedures stated at the beginning of the course were either inconsistently followed or were changed without explanation or advance notice. One could look at the situation of altering or inconsistently following the grading plan as analogous to playing a game in which the rules arbitrarily change, sometimes without the players' knowledge. The ability to participate becomes an extremely difficult and frustrating experience. Students are placed in the unreasonable position of never knowing for sure what the instructor considers important. When the rules need to be changed, all of the players must be informed (and, one hopes, be in agreement).

Guideline 5: The number of components or elements used to assign course grades should be large enough to enhance high accuracy in grading.

From a decision-making point of view, the more pieces of information available to the decision maker, the more confidence one can have that the decision will be accurate and appropriate. This same principle applies to the process of assigning grades. If only a final exam score is used to assign a course grade, the adequacy of the grade will depend on how well the test covered all the relevant aspects of course content and how typically the student performed on one specific day during a 2- to 3-hour period. Though the minimum number of tests, quizzes, papers, projects, and/or presentations needed must be course specific, each instructor must attempt to secure as much relevant data as reasonably possible to ensure that the course grade will accurately reflect each student's achievement level.

Selection of Grading Components

Grades are typically based on a number of graded components or elements. A key to the development of a defensible grading strategy is the selection of appropriate grading components. Grading components used for determining course grades should reflect each student's competence in the course content. Grading components can include such diverse indicators of student performance as exams, homework, projects, quizzes, and class participation.

There are several aspects of student performance such as class attendance, mechanics (e.g., grammar and spelling), and personality factors that should not be used for determining course grades. Grades based on these criteria simply are not defensible. For example, at the end of one semester an instructor called us about how to handle a student who was threatening to file a capricious grading charge. The instructor said he assigned the student a *B* because he never came to class so the student did not deserve an *A*. The student declared that he deserved an *A* because he performed at the *A* level on all the grading components. We were at a loss when the instructor asked us how to defend his assignment of a *B* as a course grade. The same type of problem exists when grades are based on personality factors. A student assigned a *C* should be performing at about the class average and have a moderate amount of knowledge about the course content whether he or she is agreeable or disagreeable to be around.

You may decide you want to evaluate or give students feedback on these aspects of their performance. Judgments about writing and speaking skills, personality traits, and motivations can be communicated in another form. Some instructors use brief conferences, others communicate through written comments on papers or exams.

Weighting Grading Components

Clearly some indicators of student performance should be weighted more heavily than others. For example, classroom participation is not usually weighted as heavily as performance on a classroom exam. When deciding the relative weight of each of the grading components, instructors need to consider the extent to which

- Each grading component measures important course goals
- Achievement can be accurately measured with each grading component
- Each grading component measures a different content area of course or course objectives compared with other grading components

Once the weights are determined (i.e., 3 hourly exams are weighted 20% each and the final exam is weighted 40%), applying the weights for the grading components is straightforward provided the standard deviation (the spread of scores) for each grading component is similar or standard scores are used. Standard scores are calculated by converting the original raw scores to a common scale with a predetermined mean and standard deviation. For example, our testing office provides standard scores with a mean of 500 and a standard deviation of 100. When scores are standardized, scores can be compared across tests. Most test analysis packages provide standardized scores automatically. Using standard scores for weighting grading components is the easiest way to ensure the weighting of each component is accurate.

If standard scores are not available, it is critical to determine if the standard deviations of the weighting components are

Table 7.1 An Example of Weighting Grade Components

Student	Midterm	Rank	Exam	Final Rank	Total	Rank
A	50	6	145	5	195	6
B	90	2	125	9	215	2
C	70	4	135	7	205	4
D	80	3	130	8	210	3
E	60	5	140	6	200	5
F	40	7	150	4	190	7
G	10	10	165	1	175	10
H	30	8	155	3	185	8
I	20	9	160	2	180	9
J	100	1	120	10	220	1

Statistic	Midterm	Final Exam	Total
Perfect score	100	200	300
Standard deviation	28.7	14.4	
Desired weight	1	1	
Observed weight	2	1	
Required multiplier	1	2	

different. A simple example to demonstrate the need for comparable standard deviations among graded components is presented in Table 7.1.

Given the example data in Table 7.1, suppose an instructor decides she wants a 100-point midterm and 200-point final to each count 50% of the total grade. Typically, she simply adds together the grading components. For example, student G received a 10 on the midterm and a 165 on the final for a total score of 175. However, is the 175 an accurate measure of student performance? Student G received the lowest score (Rank = 10) on the midterm and the highest score (Rank = 1) on the final. Yet student G's total score is the lowest in the class (Rank = 10). If this is noticed, many new instructors think the differences in the number of possible points on the exams is the problem. At this point they will multiply scores on the midterm by 2 so both exams are based on a possible score of 200. However, this will not solve the dilemma because the rank order of the students' scores stays the same. To resolve this problem, you should adjust the scores on the second exam so the standard deviations of the two exams are equal by multiplying each score on the final exam by 2 (14.4 × 2 = 28.8). Now each grading component contributes equal weight to the new total score.

Activity: Examine how you selected and combined weights for assigning course grading the last time you taught a course. Check to see if you used standard scores or whether the standard deviations of your grading components were similar.

Conceptual Basis for Grade Assignment and Grading Methods

Instructors must decide what the conceptual basis of their grading strategy will be. Grading entails some type of comparison. Generally, college grades reflect student competence compared with other students (normative or relative) or established standards (absolute or standards of excellence). Descriptions of both types of comparisons—normative and absolute—and the methods used to follow each philosophy are presented next.

Normative or Relative

Description. By comparing a student's overall course performance with that of some relevant group of students, the instructor assigns a grade to show the student's level of achievement or standing within that group. A C usually indicates the student tended to perform at the class average. An A is awarded to the best students. We cannot, however, say that an A represents superior achievement if the achievement level of the reference group overall is not competent. An A in this case may only identify the best of the mediocre students. The quality of the reference group is the key to interpreting grades based on normative comparisons. Examples of reference groups for college and university grading are all students currently enrolled in the class or all students who have completed the course since it was first offered.

Advantages

1. Individuals whose academic performance is outstanding compared to their peers are rewarded.
2. The strategy is a common one that many faculty members are familiar with. Given additional information about the students, instructor, or college department, grades from the strategy can be interpreted easily.

Disadvantages

1. No matter how outstanding the reference group is, some students will get low grades—and the converse is true—no matter how incompetent the reference group, some students will receive high grades.
2. Grades are difficult to interpret without information on the overall group.
3. Grading standards may fluctuate with the quality of each class of students. Grades depend on who was in the particular class. Standards are raised by the performance of a bright class and lowered by the achievement of lower-performing students.
4. Course norms need to be developed to account for more than a single class's performance. Students of an instructor who is new to the course may be at a particular disadvantage because the reference group will be small and may be atypical compared with future classes.

Methods. When you select a normative or relative approach for grading, there is a specific method we recommend for determining grade assignments. This method is widely used and can be explained easily to students. This method is particularly useful in large classes and should be used with care in small classes.

❶ Convert raw scores for each grading component to some type of standard score (wherein the standard deviation and mean are fixed).

(Your testing office may provide these at your request.) Raw scores can be used instead of the standard scores if the standard deviations of all the grading components are approximately equal. (Do not convert the grading components to letter grades or distinctions among achievement levels will disappear.)

❷ Weight the scores of each grading component before combining them into a total score. For instance if you want two exams to be each weighted 30% of the grade and the final 40%, the weights of the grading components are 0.3, 0.3, and 0.4. Another way to think about this is to triple each exam and quadruple the final.

❸ Add the weighted scores to get the total score or composite.

❹ Obtain a frequency distribution from a testing package like the one in Figure 7.1 or tally the scores by listing all possible scores and the number of students receiving each score.

❺ Use the mean and standard deviation from the test analysis to determine the grade ranges. If a B is considered the average grade, add one-half of the standard deviation to the mean to determine the top of the B range and subtract one-half of the standard deviation from the mean to calculate the bottom of the B range. Because the standard deviation of the scores in Figure 7.1 is 12 and the mean is 61, the range of scores assigned a B is 55 to 67. If standard scores are used, the score range for a B is 450 to 550. The A range is 68 to 80, and the C range is 36 to 54. Three-quarters or one standard deviation can be used to define the ranges, depending on your preference.

❻ To make decisions about borderline cases, examine the information from any fudge factors. For instance, if homework is used as a fudge factor, students who have turned in most of the assignments will have their grades shifted upward, whereas the students who did not turn in assignments are not given the benefit of the doubt.

You select the values used for determining the grade cutoffs. For instance, you can use one-quarter, one-half, or three-quarters of a standard deviation for determining the cutoffs. While this method does require your judgment, it is a systematic way to assign course grades. It can be explained easily, so it should minimize miscommunication between you and your students.

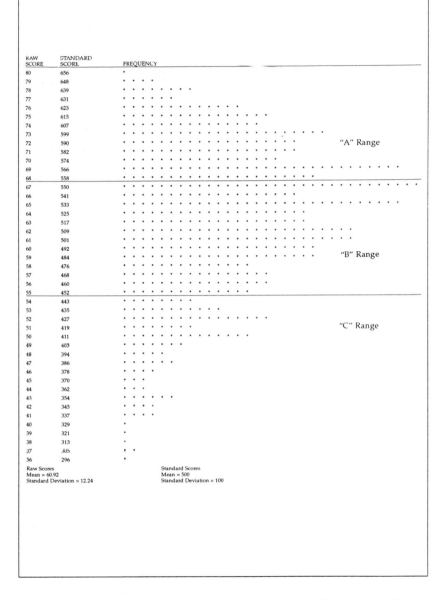

Figure 7.1. Example Frequency Distribution and Grade Cutoffs

Absolute or Standards of Excellence

Description. Grades are obtained by comparing students' performance with specified absolute standards rather than relative standards such as the work of other students. With this grading method, the goal is to determine how much of a set of tasks or content a student has mastered instead of how students perform in comparison to one another. A *C* in an introductory statistics course means the student has mastered all of the fundamental course objectives; most higher-order objectives (e.g., synthesis and evaluation) were not mastered. An *A* indicates all fundamental and higher-order objectives were achieved. With this method all students' grades depend on their mastery of the course content, not how they perform in comparison to their classmates. Theoretically, with this approach, all students can receive an *A* if all students master course goals.

Advantages
1. Course goals and standards must be clearly defined and communicated.
2. The focus is on mastery of material, not competition for a grade.
3. Final grades reflect achievement of course goals; the grades indicate what students know, not how they compare to a reference group.
4. This approach can promote a cooperative classroom climate; students do not jeopardize their own grades when they help their classmates.

Disadvantages
1. It is difficult and time-consuming to determine what course standards should be for each possible course grade.
2. The instructor has to decide on reasonable expectations of students and the necessary prerequisite knowledge for future courses, which may be particularly difficult for new instructors.
3. A complete interpretation of the meaning of a course grade cannot be made unless the major course goals are also available.

Method. When asked to recommend a basis for grading we generally prefer an absolute or standards of excellence approach. We caution how essential it is that standards are specified for this method to be defensible. We recommend the following method when using an absolute basis for grading.

❶ Using the test plan as a guide, review the test items and identify items a student with "average" knowledge of the course material will get correct. Typically, these will be items written at the knowledge or comprehension level. Add up the number of items identified as average competency items. This total number is the cutoff score for a grade of *C*, assuming a grade of *C* represents average competency.

❷ Review the items that average students are not expected to answer correctly. These are typically items written at levels higher than Bloom's comprehension level. Decide how many of these items *B* students should answer correctly. To determine the *B* to *C* grade cutoff, add the total of these items to the total identified in step 1.

❸ Determine the number of the remaining items that students need to answer correctly to obtain a grade of *A*. Add this number to the *B* cutoff score to set the *A* cutoff score.

❹ Review the items that *C* students were expected to answer correctly. Determine how many of these items should be answered correctly by a student to minimally pass the exam. This number is the *D* to *F* grade cutoff.

❺ If desired, subtract one to three points for each cutoff to account for measurement error.

❻ Convert the grades from the grading components (papers, exams, and class projects) to numbers ($A = 5$, $B = 4$, etc.). Weight the numbers according to the percentages determined at the beginning of the course, for example, the final is 40% of the grade. Average the weighted components to determine the course grades. Decisions about borderline cases are examined using achievement information from the fudge factor.

To illustrate, an instructor administered a 50-item exam. He identified 25 items that a *C* student should answer correctly. A total of 8 additional items were identified as items that should be answered correctly by B students, and an additional 9 items were noted that should be answered correctly by A students. The instructor set the minimum pass cutoff at 15. Thus the following cutoff scores were created:

A	42 to 50
B	33 to 41
C	25 to 32
D	15 to 24
F	0 to 14

Other Comparisons: Improvement and Effort

Using improvement as a basis for grading may be unfair. When grades are based on improvement, a student who initially knows a minimum amount of course material and learns quite a bit, receives a high grade. Small gains are represented by low grades. Students who enter the course with some knowledge of the course content are penalized, whereas students with minimal knowledge are at a significant advantage. Students' proficiency at the end of the course is a more useful basis for grades at the college level. Grading relative to effort is similar. In this case students who make a significant effort to learn the course material are rewarded for that effort. In contrast, students who have ability in the area and can attain course competence with minimal effort may be downgraded. The key for both of these grading comparisons involves student competence with respect to the course material. All students receiving an A in a course should have a similar grasp of the course material. When improvement and effort are used as a basis of grading, students with very different proficiency levels may all receive an A. Consequently, an A no longer means superior achievement or mastery of the course material.

Activity: Think about the last time you assigned course grades. What basis for grading was used? Were the grades assigned based on a normative or standards approach?

Other Less-Defensible Methods

The Distribution Gap Method

A common method for assigning grades is the distribution gap method. A frequency distribution or tally of scores is obtained by the instructor. The instructor conducts a visual inspection of the distribution to identify gaps in the scores. The instructor draws a horizontal line at the top of the first gap (the cutoffs for an *A*). A second gap is found for the *B* range. The process continues until ranges for all grades are identified. The major problem with this approach is how the gaps are formed. The gaps may be caused more by measurement error (guessing or poorly written test items) than levels of achievement. The occurrence of distinctive gaps is a random phenomenon. If you administered an alternate form of the test, the gaps may well appear in different places. Grade cutoffs should not be based on a random variable such as the occurrence of distinctive gaps. Furthermore, how are gap-determined grades explained to students? Do you say, "John received a *B* because there was a group of scores right above his score that looked like *A* scores"?

Grading on the Curve

Grading on the curve is based on the notion of establishing quotas for each grade category. This approach is very efficient and simple to implement. However, there is no rationale for determining what percent should get *A*'s, *B*'s, and *D*'s. Once these quotas are set grades are assigned without regard to achievement. No distinctions are made between those at the top of the top and bottom of the *A* range. There may well be a 20-point difference. The same problem exists for range assigned an *F*. If the lowest 5% of the score are assigned an *F*, there may be few differences in achievement levels between the bottom 5% and the bottom 15% of the scores.

Percent Grading

Percent grading is probably one of the oldest methods used to assign course grades. Scores on papers, tests, and projects are usually converted to a percent based on the total possible score. Typically, the percent score is interpreted as the percent of content the student has mastered. Students who receive a 93% on a test are considered to know 93% of the course material. This approach has similar problems to grading on the curve. There is no systematic way to decide what the grade ranges should be. For instance, should 90% to 100% or 93% to 100% be the *A* range? This grading method is particularly complicated when an instructor determines ahead of time that answering 90% to 100% of the items correct earns an *A* and the highest grade on the exam turns out to be 68%. The are no reasonable strategies for dealing with this kind of problem if you are using the percent grading method. One approach is to give only *D*'s and *F*'s on the exam. The other approach is to adjust the scores by making the score at 68% equivalent to 100%. However, the scores can no longer be interpreted as the percentage of content the student has mastered, and students quickly lose confidence that they are being graded fairly.

Evaluating Your Grading Strategy

If you are concerned about your grading strategies, we recommend asking for student feedback during or at the end of a course. Instructors can request feedback before the end of the course. We have included items that are typically used on an end-of-course evaluation form.

General
The grading procedures for the course were

Very fair   Very unfair
   1   2   3   4   5

Was the grading system for the course explained?

Yes, very well   No, not at all
   1   2   3   4   5

Specific
Did the instructor set too high/low a grading standard for students?

Too high   Too low
   1   2   3   4   5

How would you characterize the instructor's grading system?

Very objective   Very subjective
   1   2   3   4   5

The amount of graded feedback given to me during the course was

Quite adequate   Not enough
   1   2   3   4   5

Were requests for regrading or review handled fairly?

Yes, almost always   No, almost never
   1   2   3   4   5

The instructor evaluated my work in a meaningful and conscientious manner.

Strongly agree   Strongly disagree
   1   2   3   4   5

We have always found grading workshops to be the most challenging training activities because instructors want to know the best way to assign grades. No best way exists. We have tried to indicate our preferences in this section. We believe some methods are better than others for particular situations. Probably the best test of any approach or method is whether or not you can both explain it and defend it to your students. If you have trouble doing one or the other or both, you may want to reexamine your grading preferences.

8 | Twelve Activities for Classroom Testing and Grading

We have presented classroom testing and grading as a process involving a number of teaching activities, including developing course objectives, writing test items, administering exams, reviewing test quality, scoring exams, and awarding grades. The following activities are interrelated so that completion of one is dependent on or influences the completion of another. In Table 8.1 we have tried to summarize the contents of this book while illustrating our testing development and review process. The process is reviewed below.

Activity 1: The process begins by (1) identifying desired student achievements through the development of course objectives and (2) specifying content areas covered in the course. We commonly expect student achievement at several levels of learning, for example, knowledge of information and application of knowledge.

Activity 2: Develop a testing plan that provides appropriate coverage of content and course objectives while addressing your needs and the needs of your students. The plan should address questions such as, How many exams will be given? of what type? of what

Table 8.1 Test Development and Review Process

Activity 1	Identify test content areas and develop course objectives
Activity 2	Develop a testing plan
Activity 3	Develop test specifications by selecting critical objectives and content
Activity 4	Write or select test items to meet test specifications
Activity 5	Conduct a preliminary review of test items
Activity 6	Assemble test form(s)
Activity 7	Administer tests
Activity 8	Evaluate test and item performance
Activity 9	Identify and handle problem items
Activity 10	Plan to review or reteach troublesome content areas
Activity 11	Make item revisions and enter good and revised items into an item file
Activity 12	Score tests and assign grades

length? for what purpose? How will you administer, score, and grade exams? How will you use test results? How will your students be able to use their results?

Activity 3: Not all content or objectives can be tested without taking a substantial amount of classroom time away from instruction. Develop a test blueprint (or test specifications) by selecting critical objectives and content to be tested. Follow the blueprint to ensure that you are testing what you are teaching.

Activity 4: Write test items—or select items from old exams, item banks, or textbook item files—to match the objectives and content areas identified in the test specifications. Items and matching course objectives should require student achievement at the same level of learning.

Activity 5: Before test administration, conduct a preliminary review of test items written or selected to identify those that fail to follow rules for writing test items, may be confusing, or are too easy or too hard.

Activity 6: Following a review of the test items, assemble them into one or two test forms. Provide directions on the forms that tell students of the type of response desired, the manner in which responses should be made, and other appropriate information. Exams should be professional in appearance, free from typing errors, spaced properly on the page, and without inappropriate page breaks within test items.

Activity 7: Administer exams with consideration to possible student problems or acts of dishonesty. Share with the entire class important student questions asked during the exam. Follow procedures to discourage the occurrence of cheating, for example, staggered seating, identification numbers on exams, and/or adequate proctoring.

Activity 8: Evaluate both the quality of the test and the test items following test administration. Compute test statistics (mean, standard error, and reliability) and item statistics (difficulty and discrimination indices) to evaluate how well the test and items performed. Were the items confusing and misunderstood? Were the items too difficult or too easy? Did they discriminate among students of different achievement levels?

Activity 9: Handle problem items identified in the review process appropriately. Confusing items can be eliminated from the test or multiple correct answers can be identified. Discuss problem items with the class during an in-class review of the exam.

Activity 10: What were the problem items? Did they cover the same content area or test a particular group of objectives? Consider reviewing and/or reteaching troublesome content.

Activity 11: The test review identified good items, poor items, and items needing minor revision. After making the necessary revisions to some of the items, place good and improved items into an item file or bank for future use. Subsequent testing situations will be made easier by accumulating items of proven quality.

Activity 12: After handling problem items, rescore the exam papers and assign grades accordingly. Grades should be awarded fairly and accurately as possible. You should be able to explain and defend your basis for grading.

Final Words

You can develop excellent classroom assessment procedures by following these 12 activities. Developing well-prepared tests and well-planned grading procedures should give you a sense of confidence that you are making your best effort to evaluate the efforts of your students. It should also improve your teaching, which, according to research on student ratings of instruction, will not go unnoticed by your appreciative students.

Practical Approaches to Dealing With Cheating on Exams

INSTRUCTIONAL & MANAGEMENT SERVICES
INSTRUCTIONAL DEVELOPMENT DIVISION

University of Illinois at Urbana-Champaign | No. 4

PRACTICAL APPROACHES TO DEALING WITH CHEATING ON EXAMS

It is the responsibility of faculty to discourage students from cheating and not turn their back on cheating when it is detected. To meet both responsibilities, faculty need to carefully plan classroom and testing procedures which take into account the many ways in which cheating occurs, and learn how to follow institutional guidelines when imposing a penalty.

What are the responsibilities of faculty and students?

At the University of Illinois at Urbana-Champaign, the booklet, Code on Campus Affairs and Regulations Applying to All Students, is published prior to each fall semester. It is available without charge from the Office of Admissions and Records, 177 Administration Building, to all staff members and students. The Code contains the University's definition of cheating and the campus policies and guidelines for dealing with its occurrence. It is valuable to read it thoroughly before beginning instruction each semester or when writing and administering exams and quizzes.

In the August 1986 edition, Rule 64 of the Code presents the university's statement on academic integrity which pertains to all students and faculty members. In the preamble of this section it is stated that:

"The University has the responsibility for maintaining the academic integrity so as to guard the quality of scholarship on our campus and to protect those who depend on our knowledge and integrity. It is the responsibility of the student to refrain from academic dishonesty, to re-frain from conduct which may lead to suspicion of academic dishonesty, and to refrain from conduct which aids others in academic dishonesty."

All instructors are responsible for the establishment and maintenance of an environment which supports academic integrity and prevents academic dishonesty.

How do students cheat?

Students cheat on exams in different and creative ways.

For example, imagine a common setting where a multiple-choice exam is being administered to students in a lecture hall or classroom. The students are instructed to sit anywhere they wish but in every other seat. The following forms of cheating have been documented:

1. Two students sitting one desk apart share an eraser. The students write answers on the eraser and pass it back and forth.

2. Students write pertinent information on the visors of their caps, shirt cuffs, or the palms of their hands.

135

3. Students wear a 'walkman' portable radio with headphones) which has recordings of pertinent information.

4. Students store answers on hand calculators, then use and/or share the calculators with other students.

5. Students arrange themselves at locations and angles so that they can easily pass information. Some of these arrangements include:

   a. the 'power wedge' where students form a triangle with the knowledgeable student at the bottom point. Other participating students sit at higher levels, fanning out as the rows go upward;

   b. students sitting one seat apart but with pertinent books and papers placed on top of the separating desk;

   c. students sitting close enough to look at each other's exams.

6. Students use a code system such as tapping or hand signals to communicate back and forth.

7. 'Ghost' persons, knowledgeable in the subject, take the exam by impersonating the real student.

8. Students appear to take the exam but do not turn one in. Later the students accuse the instructor of losing the exams and demand to be given a re-test or amenable grades.

9. One student creates a diversion by asking a question of the proctor so that the proctor cannot observe other students cheating.

10. Both a 'ghost' person and the enrolled student take the exam. The 'ghost' person puts the student's name on the exam and completes it. The student takes the exam but puts a fictitious name on it. Both exams are turned in. In the end, the instructor has no alternative but to discard the extra exam.

11. Two forms (A & B) of the exam are handed out. Students, who have gotten the answers to Form A prior to the test, may be given Form B. The students are instructed to code the answer sheet with whichever exam form they were given. These students code in Form 'A' instead of 'B' and then provide the answers they have previously gotten.

What can faculty do?

Advance Communication

Whatever decisions faculty make regarding academic integrity, *it is imperative that full communication ahead of time and during the exam takes place between faculty members and their proctors.*

Faculty need to make a clear statement on the first day of class about procedures that follow. This statement can also appear in the course syllabus, be repeated the class day before an exam, and/or as an exam begins.

Some suggested procedures for test preparation and test administration follow.

Test Preparation

1. Prepare more than one form of the exam. Possible alternatives are to have the same questions on each form but:

   a. present questions in different orders;

   b. vary the orders of the response alternatives;

   c. modify values within the same question on different forms so that responses are different (essentially parallel items may be useful where calculations are involved).

2. Pre-code answer sheets and test booklets by:

   a. using a numbering system so that the number on each test booklet matches the one on each student's answer sheet;

   b. marking the answer sheets in such a way that the coding cannot be altered, e.g., by using a 'Sharpie' felt-tip pen.

Test Administration

1. Most cheating on tests in large classes occurs when students are allowed to sit wherever they choose. It should be no surprise that cheaters choose to sit near each other! By numbering seats and tests and

then assigning students with a test to sit in the seat with the same number, cheating can be greatly minimized. Seating arrangements are effective if they are a surprise to the test takers! Students should be warned that penalties will follow if seating directions are not followed.

2. Be systematic in handing out alternate forms, assuring the alternate order. Take into account students sitting laterally as well as those sitting in front and in back of each other.

3. Always attempt to have sufficient proctors for the exam. It is hard to pick an exact ratio, but one proctor per 40 students, when the proctor does not know the students, is advisable. If the proctor does know the students, e.g., as a quiz instructor, then having the students sit together by section in preassigned seats, is advisable. This latter assists in minimizing 'ghost' exam takers because it is easier for the proctors to recognize and account for their own students.

4. When the identity of the exam takers is a concern, require students to bring their student I.D. and another form of identification to each exam. Of course, this only works if proctors carefully look at each I.D. and student!

5. Have an enrollment list or card file of names or signatures to be matched against I.D.s or exam answer sheets and checked off as the students enter (or leave) the exam room.

6. Proctors should be alert, moving around the exam room. They should not be reading or involved in unnecessary chatter with other proctors. They should never leave the students alone.

7. Any suspicious conduct by the students should be attended to _immediately._ If any conduct is suspicious (but not necessarily conclusive), you should move the students to other locations in the room. This is most successful when it is done immediately and with as little disturbance as possi-

ble. State ahead of time that you plan to follow this practice when something suspicious occurs, and that you do it as an assistance to all students involved. A statement such as this frequently helps to reduce the disturbance element.

What can you do when cheating occurs?

Charging students with cheating may not be the easiest thing you have ever done, but if you have followed the suggestions in this document, you will have an easier time than will faculty members who were less prepared. Having taken adequate preventive measures, you have fulfilled your responsibility for maintaining academic integrity and should consider the following suggestions when charging students:

1. **Be certain** that you are acting fairly and objectively and have all the facts.

2. Become familiar with the campus code (Rule 64 in the Code) to know the procedures to follow. The UIUC ombudsman (3-1345) is one resource for assisting you through this process. The Executive Director of the Senate Subcommittee on Student Discipline (3-0050) is another resource.

3. Speak with:
   a. your department head or chair to learn of departmental and college practices;
   b. other faculty, especially those in your department to see what they have done, and what has resulted when they have charged students with cheating.

5. Become familiar with the sanction alternatives, and at what level of these alternatives students' appeals leave your departmental jurisdiction.

6. Be able to justify the sanction you wish to impose, attempting to match it with the level or type of cheating that has taken place.

7. When your proctors or teaching assistants wish to make a charge of cheating, learn the facts surround-

ing their charge, and support them in pursuing appropriate action.

8. Do not make threats to students that you or the University cannot back up. For instance, once you have charged cheating, do not tell students that you are going to "flunk them and kick them out of school." Rule 64 in the Code states that while UIUC faculty have the independent authority to give reduced or failing grades on assignments and exams, and in a course, they can only recommend a suspension or dismissal! By being knowledgeable about the Code, you can be better assured of commenting appropriately to students.

9. Remember that a system for appealing all sanctions has been established for all students.

Remember: The UIUC Code states that once you are aware that cheating has occurred, you have a responsibility to make a charge. Your responsibility extends to all of your students who do not cheat, as well as to your colleagues and teaching assistants.

What takes place when you take action?

Once you have formally charged a student with cheating, the UIUC process is set in motion. When students decide to appeal the charge, we urge you to continually communicate with your department head as the appeal process moves through its stages. Knowing what is in the Code is essential. Listed below are additional thoughts.

• All students at the UIUC (and most institutions of higher learning) have the opportunity to appeal charges of cheating.

• Prepare yourself for moments of uneasy feelings. These are common and do not mean that you have made a mistake or are being unreasonable. These moments may also occur well after the entire procedure is over.

• Support your teaching assistants/proctors in handling the pressures incurred. They will be looking to you for guidance more so at this time than at any other.

FINAL WORDS

It is much easier for students to meet their obligations for academic integrity when faculty create conditions which minimize cheating, and deal fairly with cheating when it does occur.

ADDITIONAL HELP

The Instructional Development (3-3370) and Measurement and Evaluation (3-3490) Divisions of the Office of Instructional and Management Services at the University of Illinois at Urbana-Champaign are campus-wide units which work with faculty, departments and colleges to promote effective instruction.

For further information contact:
Instructional Development Division
307 Engineering Hall
1308 W. Green St., Urbana, IL 61801
217-333-3370 or 3490
MGH/JO:87

SOURCE: Published by and used by permission from the Office of Instructional Resources, Division of Instructional Development, University of Illinois at Urbana-Champaign, 1987.

References

Bloom, B. S., Engelhart, M. D., Furst, E. J., Hill, W. H., & Krathwohl, D. R. (1956). *Taxonomy of educational objectives: The classification of educational goals.* New York: David McKay.

Carlson, S. B. (1985). *Creative classroom testing.* Princeton, NJ: Educational Testing Service.

Ebel, R. L. (1972). *Essentials of educational measurement.* Englewood Cliffs, NJ: Prentice-Hall.

Ebel, R. L., & Frisbie, D. A. (1991). *Essentials of educational measurement* (5th ed.). Englewood Cliffs, NJ: Prentice-Hall.

Educational Testing Service. (1987). *Sensitivity review process.* Princeton, NJ: Educational Testing Service.

Gronlund, N. E., & Linn, R. L. (1990). *Measurement and evaluation in teaching* (6th ed.). New York: Macmillan.

Hogan, T. P. (1981). *Relationship between free-response and choice type tests of achievement: A review of the literature.* (ERIC Document Reproduction Service, No. ED 224 811)

McKeachie, W. J. (1986). *Teaching tips: A guidebook for the beginning college teacher.* Lexington, MA: Heath.

National Evaluation Systems, Inc. (1987). *Bias issues in test development.* Amherst, MA: Author.

Office of Instructional Resources. (1979). *Assigning course grades.* Champaign: University of Illinois at Urbana-Champaign.

Patterson, D. C. (1926). Do new and old type examinations measure different material functions? *School and Society, 24,* 246.

Smallwood, M. L. (1935). *An historical study of examinations and grading systems in early American universities.* Cambridge, MA: Harvard University Press.

Weller, D. L. (1983) The grading nemesis: An historical overview and a current look at pass/fail grading. *Journal of Research and Development in Education, 17,* 39-45.

About the Authors

John C. Ory is the Director of the Office of Instructional Resources and Associate Professor in the Department of Educational Psychology at the University of Illinois at Urbana-Champaign. He received his Ph.D. in Educational Psychology at the University of Kansas. His research interests are in student assessment and faculty evaluation. He has coauthored *Evaluating Teaching Effectiveness*. He has conducted more than 100 workshops and seminars on classroom testing and grading at community colleges, universities, public schools, and corporate training centers.

Katherine E. Ryan received her Ph.D. from the University of Illinois, Urbana-Champaign. She is currently Associate Head of the Division of Measurement and Evaluation in the Office of Instructional Resources and an Assistant Professor in the Department of Educational Psychology at the University of Illinois at Urbana-Champaign. She has conducted workshops on test development and grading practices for postsecondary, secondary, and elementary education audiences. Her research interests include item bias, alternative test item formats, performance assessment, and ethnic and gender differences in educational achievement.